Ste
Co

and
Diesel Locomotive
Fueling Facilities

by

Thomas W. Dixon, Jr.

The 1,000-ton Coaling Station at Russell, Ky. is framed by two of the Chesapeake & Ohio's massive locomotives while others gather under it like chicks under a hen, in the wartime summer of 1943.

(C&O Railway photo, C&O Historical Society collection)

*Published 2002 by
TLC Publishing Inc.
1387 Winding Creek Lane
Lynchburg, Virginia 24503-3776*

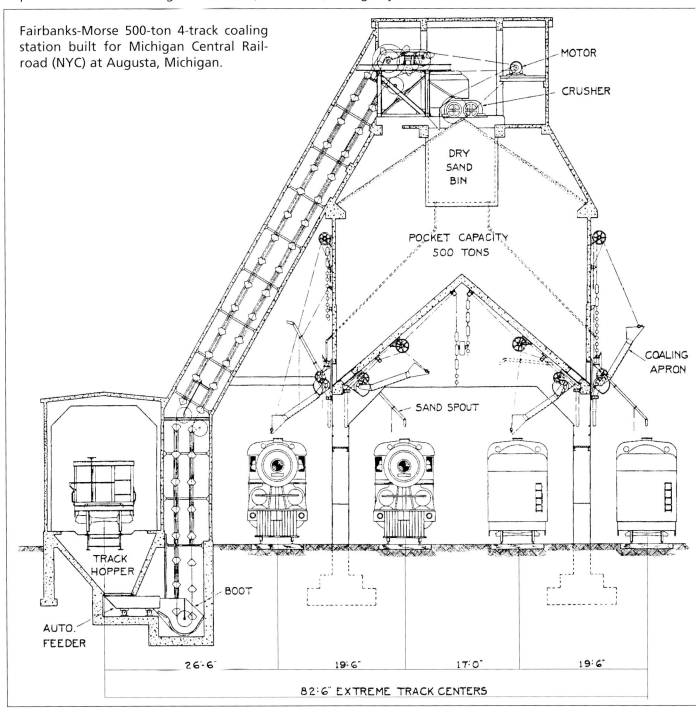

Fairbanks-Morse 500-ton 4-track coaling station built for Michigan Central Railroad (NYC) at Augusta, Michigan.

MOTOR

CRUSHER

DRY SAND BIN

POCKET CAPACITY 500 TONS

COALING APRON

SAND SPOUT

TRACK HOPPER

BOOT

AUTO. FEEDER

26'-6"   19'-6"   17'-0"   19'-6"

82'-6" EXTREME TRACK CENTERS

ISBN 1-883089-77-8

Library of Congress Catalog Card Number: 2001096304

(*Right*) So much of railroading was done at night, but it was so little photographed. The few available photos are, however, dramatic. This photo above shows night activity at NKP's Conneaut, Ohio engine terminal with the coaling station and cinder conveyor framing one of the line's famous Berkshire 2-8-4s.

(John Rehor)

Table of Contents

The towering coaling station was one of the great icons of the steam age, at least for the railroad employees and engine crews. This night photo of a Nickel Plate Road Pacific type and others huddling around the Frankfort, Indiana coaling station in 1945, carries evocations of the Romance and lure of steam railroading.
(Richard Cook photo, Jay Williams Collection)

Introduction

The purpose of this small book is to explain and give examples of how steam locomotives and early diesel-electric locomotives were supplied with fuel, and in the case of steam, how the residue of combustion (ash) was disposed. It is aimed first at setting a historical context for these often huge structures that dominated railroad terminals and yards for so many years, even up to the present. Secondly, it presents illustrations and examples of what some of the major styles looked like and how they worked, for the benefit of model railroaders.

This is not intended to be a complete historical monograph about this subject, nor a catalog of the types and builders, because the subject is so large it will not permit it within an economically reasonable space.

I have chosen to lift excerpts directly from several different issues of contemporary professional railroad publications, catalogs and advertisements of the major builders of these facilities, and to interweave them with some photos of actual in-service installations, showing locomotives bustling around.

"Portrait" style photos of the coaling stations are fairly hard to find, though they appear in many photos as background, so you'll find some of both. If there seems to be an unusual amount of photos showing C&O facilities, it's because that road happens to be my area of expertise, and I have access to the greatest number of photos and drawings that would pertain.

Some roads preferred one builder or another, while others bought the coaling stations from several builders, and still others built their own from scratch. However, usually, the major builders were responsible for probably 90% of the installations in the period after about 1910.

Some background discussion of operations in the late 19th and early 20th Centuries is needed, but the preponderance of attention is given to the 1920s-1950s era for steam and the 1950s era for diesels.

Many photos have been lifted from old publications and therefore will not have the clarity of the ones taken directly from good quality photographic prints and negatives.

The idea for this book came from the modeling community. Although I am not a modeler, about everyone I deal with in the railroad interest organization, history, and book business is. This long association has resulted in my becoming more appreciative of how prototype facilities, installations, and operations are usually portrayed by modelers. I have become aware that modelers have the potential to be the principal preservers of the American railway heritage. Adherents and practitioners of the fairly recent movement called "prototype modeling" take the attitude that they want to recreate the scene and operations as accurately as possible. This is a departure from the earlier period when modeling was viewed in more generic terms. That's why I believe that there is more and more a convergence of goals for the historian and the modeler. Among those operations that seem to me to get less than their fair share of attention in modeling are: fueling stations, water stations, mail and express facilities/operations, and passenger train makeup and operation. This book is an attempt to give more perspective to the fueling stations aspect.

I have contributed very little real knowledge to the subject, but rather have edited and selected the images to portray and have analyzed the material as well as I could.

I appreciate especially the kind assistance from Jay Williams, John B. Corns, Ken Miller, Kevin Holland, Pat Dorin, the C&O Historical Society Collection, Jim Gillum and the N&W Historical Society, for their help in this endeavor.

Thomas W. Dixon, Jr.
Lynchburg, Virginia, June 2002

The Coaling Station and Its Function

A coaling station is simply a location on the railroad designated for the placing of coal into locomotive tender. Before coal came into widespread use as a locomotive fuel, wood was used, and in that era the wood was simply piled up alongside the track on an elevated platform, and piled into the tender's fuel bunker by hand. As coal came into use, these same simple, uncomplicated but very inefficient and labor intensive operations continued in use. However, as locomotives became much larger and their capacities to carry fuel greatly expanded, other methods had to be devised.

Gravity and the chute became the accepted way to coal locomotives. But for gravity to be used, the coal had to be placed above the locomotive tender. This led to the early use of the ramp-style coaling station, where cars of coal were pushed up an incline to bunkers positioned well above the height of the locomotive tenders. The coal was then dumped into these bunkers and held until needed, at which time a chute was lowered and the coal allowed to fall out. In the late 19th Century and early 20th Century this became the most common, but by no means the only, way that coal was delivered to locomotives. Many of these facilities were replaced over the years with later designs but some persisted to the end of steam.

Other methods included the use of a conveyor belt of some type lifting coal from a pile on the ground up to the tender bunker, or use of a clam-shell bucket on a crane to move the coal from a car into the tender, and yet, sometimes, manually by men with shovels.

Gradually the idea of the bunker with chutes positioned above the engine terminal was refined to do away with the large ramp, which had many disadvantages, not the least of which was the amount of space it occupied. The new method was to elevate the coal above the locomotives in a freestanding bunker with chutes. These bunkers were first made of large wooden beams and planks fitted with the necessary hardware for delivery of the coal. These structures could allow locomotives to coal directly beneath and/or to either side of the main structure, which was elevated on legs or columns. This took up very little

space and was quite efficient in delivering the coal rapidly. But, the coal had to be elevated into the bunker, which was usually accomplished by a skip-jack bucket arrangement that used dump-buckets traveling independently up and down a set of tracks, dumping coal from a pit into the hopper above the tracks. The other method was a heavy bucket-conveyor. These systems required a steam or electrical motor to pull the heavy loads upward. Electric hoisting machinery was almost always used and was usually located in an elevator house or monitor at the top of the structure or near the unloading pit on the ground; the skip-jack bucket arrangement or conveyor bucket elevator being located to one side or the other.

By 1906 the reinforced concrete coaling station had made its appearance. In concept it was exactly like the wooden predecessor, but the wooden superstructure was replaced with concrete. This provided not only a stronger structure, but one that experienced little deterioration from the elements, which had always plagued the wooden structures. Some wooden stations lasted to the end of steam, but they were a decided minority.

By the 1920s almost all new installations were of the concrete type, with several large companies specializing in building and equipping them for the various railroads. The largest companies engaged in this work were the Roberts & Schaefer Company, the Ogle Construction Company, and Fairbanks Morse Company. Other players in this business included the Ross & White Company, and the Howlett Construction Company.

The concrete bunker usually contained various segmented hoppers within its superstructure, into which different grades and types of coal could be deposited for specific uses. See pages 10 and 11 for detailed drawings of how the C&O coaling station at Thurmond, W. Va. worked on the inside. This station used a conveyor bucket system rather than the skip-jack buckets and was quite typical in its layout and design.

As the locomotive stood under one of the chutes, the fireman would pull a dispensing chain which allowed the coal to tumble into a chute and to be

Not much dwafs the Norfolk and Western Class A, but the coal wharf (N&W term) at Shaffers Crossing in Roanoke, Va. does as good a job as any might.
(N&W Photo/K. L. Miller Collection)

the need for the huge superstructure, cutting down on cost and saving space. But, it required coal to be held in cars until needed, and was fairly slow in comparison with coal falling out of a huge container, both of which were disadvantages.

In a few cases coal was taken on by locomotives directly from private coal mines, if the line was located in the coal fields. This arrangement was sometimes a backup measure for emergencies, but rarely an established procedure, obviating the need for the railroad to operate or maintain a coaling station at all.

The size of coaling stations varied widely based on the particular need. About 50 tons storage capacity was the lower limit, while 1,500-2,000 tons was at the very high end. Most stations ranged in the 300-800-ton capacity for major railroads. Some of the smaller bunker style stations were built of steel rather than concrete, but they are relatively scarce since steel had the maintenance and weathering problems that concrete generally avoided for longer periods of time.

Because these structures stood over a hundred feet high, they dominated most railroad yards and terminals. The concrete structures were so solidly built that they were retained after the end of steam and were often used as platforms for lighting or continued as structures to support sanding pipes for diesels. The cost of removing these massive structures was so great that even if there were no further use for them, they were "retired in place" and left to stand derelict. In the 1990s some railroads began to remove some of the stations because their concrete was becoming brittle. Yet, at the opening of the 21st Century, many of these huge old reminders of the steam age still stand.

A few coaling stations were located away from terminals along mainlines in open country if the consumption of coal mandated a between-terminal replenishment or for use in emergencies. Although it was common for water stations to be at many spots along the route because locomotives used there their water more quickly than the coal, coaling stations were relatively rare.

deflected over an apron into the tender bunker. A second chain allowed him to stop the flow of coal. Heavy counterweights supplied the force necessary to activate the coal gates. The brakeman would signal the engineer so that the locomotive could be moved beneath the chute to fill the tender's bunker evenly.

Since it was usually necessary to replenish the sand boxes on locomotives while they were fueled, the sanding pipes were often attached to the coaling station's superstructure and the sand could flow down from an elevated bunker or be blown through them. Frequently the sand storage and drying facilities were located in the coaling station's main superstructure, while in others there was a separate storage and drying house. However, sanding facilities were not always located with the coaling station, but might have stood alone some distance away, but always in the line of service for each locomotive as it moved through the engine servicing area.

Sometimes machines called "automatic coalers" were used. Rather than having coal stored in a large bunker, the automatic station was essentially just a permanent conveyor bucket system that lifted coal out of a pit and directly into the tender. In this system a coal hopper car was simply placed over the put, the hopper doors opened and the coal allowed to flow into the pit, where the automatic coaler bucket picked it up and conveyed it into the tender. This eliminated

Early Coaling Stations

Represented below are drawings from *Buildings and Structures of American Railroads,* by Walter G. Berg, published in 1900. This book was a compilation of typical structures from numerous railroads, and was often referred to by railroad engineering departments. As a result, one is able to observe a single design, sometimes with minor variants, appearing on many railroads. Berg devotes considerable space to coaling stations, and reproduces some drawings of various types that he found in use at the turn of the 20th Century. Some of these interesting devices are reproduced below. The elevated bunker already was becoming common by this time, but many other types were also used. Berg's text concentrates very heavily on the efficiency of the operation based on the amount of time required to coal a locomotive (turn-around time in modern parlance), and the cost per ton of coal delivered. He was also concerned with the number of times the coal was handled or transferred for these reasons and also because of the breakage of the coal.

(*right*) This is a derrick coaling station on the Northern Pacific which used a stationary crane-and-bucket system. Cars delivered the coal to the platform, it was then shoveled into tipping buckets on a narrow-gauge railroad, they were then positioned around the derrick, and when needed, lifted out over the tender and dumped.
(*Berg, page 142*)

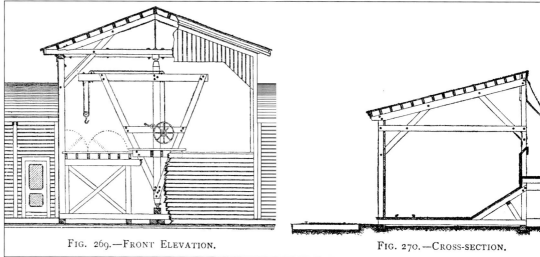

FIG. 269.—FRONT ELEVATION.

FIG. 270.—CROSS-SECTION.

(*right*) Another Northern Pacific design has the delivery of coal from hopper cars on the top, to narrow gauge hopper bottom cars, which are run out on a counterbalanced platform drawbridge and dumped into the tender.
(*Berg page 152*)

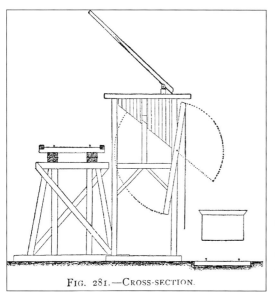

FIG. 281.—CROSS-SECTION.

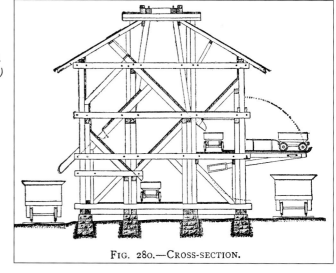

FIG. 280.—CROSS-SECTION.

(*left*) This was a standard Wabash facility. Coal was shoveled from cars on the supply track into coal pockets. The lower end of the pocket was closed by a counter-balanced apron and trap door operated by a long lever arm. The standard called for 10 pockets but could be varied depending on need.

(*Berg, page 152*)

This Lehigh Valley coaling platform, at Lehighton, Pa. was designed by Berg himself. Coal was transferred from cars on the delivery track in the rear of the elevated platform by means of moveable hand trucks and barrows and dumped through fixed revolving aprons to tenders below.

(Berg, page 146)

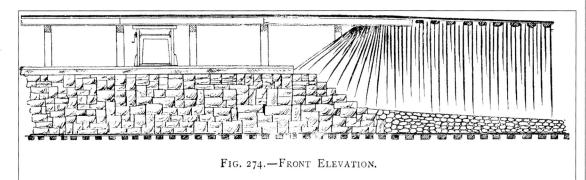

FIG. 274.—FRONT ELEVATION.

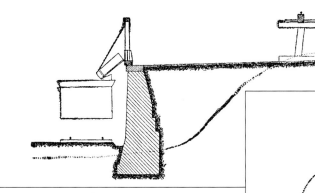

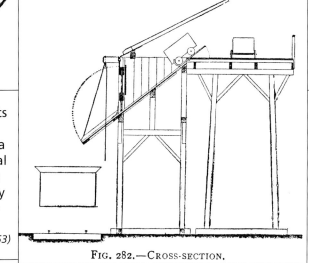

FIG. 282.—CROSS-SECTION.

The Wabash had this coaling station designed by its resident engineer. It allowed cars from the Black Diamond coal mine to discharge coal directly into a series of pockets or chutes along the track. The coal in the pockets was then discharged into tenders as needed using the long lever, in much the same way as shown on the previous page. This is an example of a coaling station at a coal mine.

(Berg, page 153)

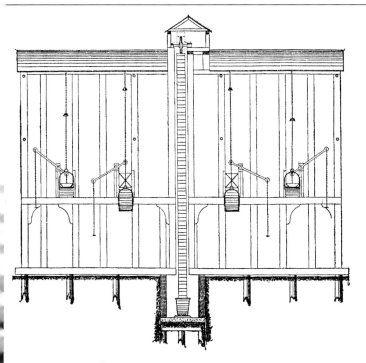

FIG. 285.—FRONT ELEVATION.

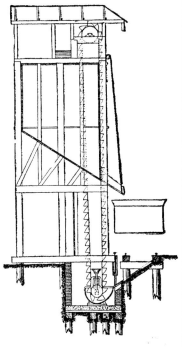

FIG. 286.—CROSS-SECTION.

This mechanical coaling station for the National Docks Railway at Jersey City, N. J., begins to look like modern facilities, with its chain bucket loader, above-track hopper storage, and apron-chute delivery system. It was a timber structure 14x50 by 34 feet high, with a bin storage capacity of 200 tons.

(Berg page 157)

Chesapeake & Ohio, Thurmond W. Va.

In this section are reproduced dimensioned drawings showing the Chesapeake & Ohio 500-ton Coaling Station (built by Fairbanks Morse in 1922) at its small, but important, Thurmond, W. Va. terminal. The drawings were made by the National Historic Engineering Record, a part of the National Park Service, and include details of how the station worked inside in a manner much clearer than actual engineering drawings, which are cluttered with the detailed dimensions, and instructions that were needed for the actual construction work. (A full set of these drawing at full size (each sheet about 2x3 feet in size) is available as part of a package of drawings showing all C&O structures at Thurmond and can be ordered from the C&O Historical Society by calling 1-800-453-COHS). This structure is still standing as of 2002.

WEST ELEVATION

NORTH ELEVATION

FEET

METERS

The station had undercut gates with hooded aprons, which pivoted 7-1/2 feet laterally so a large tender could be fully loaded with one spotting of the locomotive. The cut-off gates closed by gravity.

Constructed of reinforced concrete, the fact that this structure is still standing in relatively good condition is a testament to concrete as the preferred material for these facilities.

These sections show the internal workings of the Thurmond coaling station, including the bucket elevator (the buckets were riveted to heavy steel chain plates) pulled by an electric motor in the monitor to carry the buckets, and the bins within the main body of the structure. Cars of incoming coal entered the center track and dumped to a conveyor belt which took the coal to a crusher, then delivered it to the pit where the bucket elevator picked it up. Locomotives were coaled on either side.

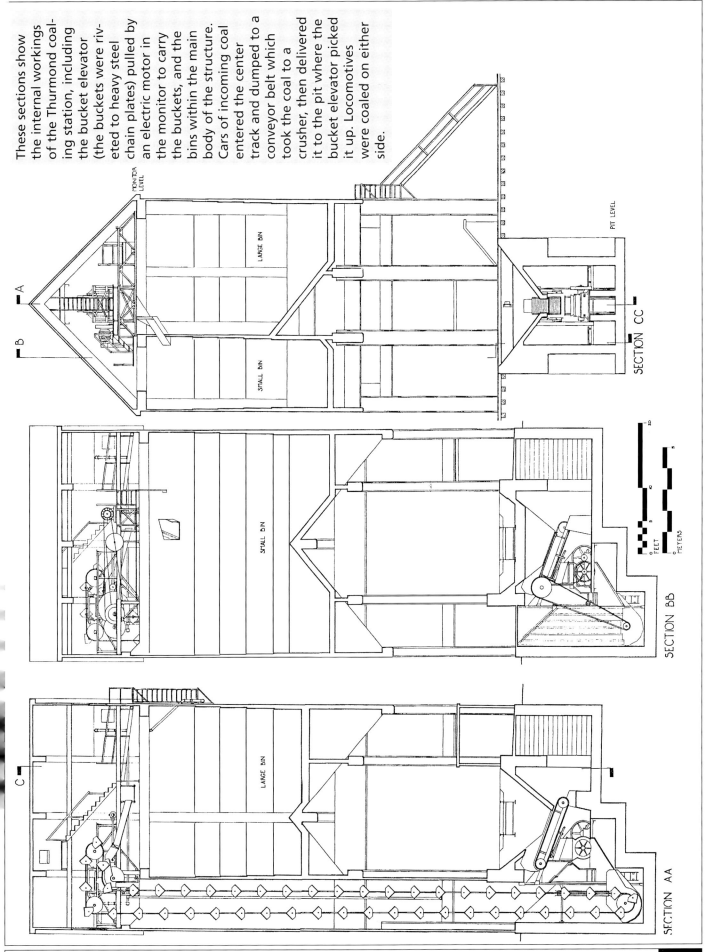

MONITOR LEVEL

A

B

LARGE BIN

SMALL BIN

SECTION CC

PIT LEVEL

SMALL BIN

SECTION BB

FEET
METERS

C

LARGE BIN

SECTION AA

Modern Coaling Stations with Wooden Superstructures

This section will look at two types of coaling stations that were built at least through the 1930s, many of which lasted to the end of steam. Both used wood as the primary material for construction of their superstructures. These facilities are divided into two styles: The first are those that I call the "wharf" style, where the coal is delivered to pockets or bins by cars on an inclined trestle track above the bins, and subsequently dumped into locomotive tenders on an even lower level. In the second type, the hopper bins are elevated above tracks on columns, with the coal being delivered to the hopper or bin by a conveyor or bucket system, then dumped through chutes to tenders below. These rightly can be called "towers." The older wharf style are really carry-overs from the 19th century styles briefly mentioned before in the section on Walter Berg's work. The wooden towers are almost exactly like the reinforced concrete structures that were the predominating facility in the final quarter century of steam operations. The concrete towers took the basic design of the wooden towers and simply re-engineered it using the different, longer lasting and essentially maintenance-free material, and will be illustrated in the next section. It is doubtful wooden facilities were built new on major railroads beyond the 1920s, but some were in service to the end of steam.

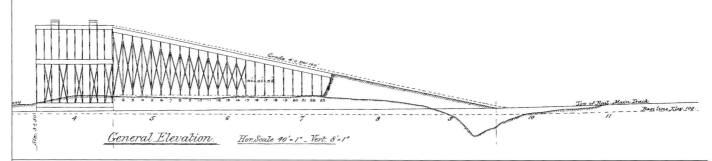

Typical of late 19th Century coaling station of the inclined ramp type (which I call "wharf") was this structure built by C&O at Providence Forge, Va. in 1887. Variations of this general arrangement continued to be built for a long time. The major disadvantage was the necessity for a great deal of space, which tended to become scarcer, especially in urban terminals.
(From C&O Drawing 318, C&O Historical Society Collection)

Although the railroad and location aren't identified, this photo of inclined trestle style coaling station appeared in the 1929 edition of *Railway Engineering & Maintenance Cyclopedia.*

his Wheeling & Lake Erie inclined trestle at Cleveland, was photographed surrounded by 0-6-0, 0-8-0 and 2-8-4 locomotives on November 11, 1946. It vividly illustrates the style, with a very steep incline up which cars had to be pushed o charge the tender coaling bins.
(Jay Williams Collection)

(right) Nickel Plate 2-8-4 No. 823 is taking on fuel at the Brewster, Ohio coal wharf in 1939. Another typical inclined trestle facility which lasted into the late era.
(Duane Bearsy photo, Jay Williams Collection)

Southern Railway 2-8-8-2 Mallet No. 4018 takes a load of coal from the wharf at Appalachia, Virginia, in December 1936.
(Paul Eilenberger, Jay Williams Collection)

Detail of what is obviously a huge Great Northern coal wharf at an unknown location in the 1920s shows the relative crudeness of this type of facility. The coal simply cascaded out of its bin into the tender, and the fireman then had to arrange it as best he could.
(TLC Publishing Collection)

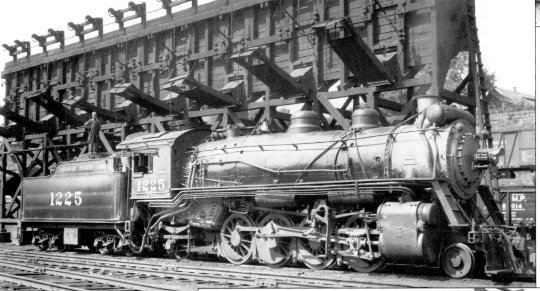

Somewhat of a hybrid, this Missouri Pacific coaling station does not use the inclined trestle for delivery of coal to its bins, but apparently lifts it by some mechanical means which isn't evident in the photo. It has the modern aprons and chutes. Space is saved by elimination of the cumbersome inclined track.
(Jay Williams Collection

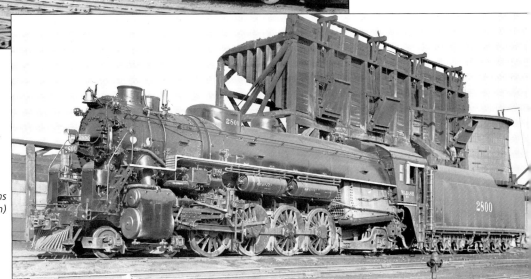

Similar to the above, a Wabash facility at Brooklyn, Illinois is fueling one of the road's M-1 class 4-8-2 on May 21, 1933.
(R. J. Foster photo, Jay Williams Collection)

Another of the wharf designs without the inclined track is this tall Norfolk & Western plant at Crewe, Virginia, with one of the road's famous A-class 2-8-8-4s (No. 1216) taking on fuel in March 1956. The large weatherboarded structure closest is the elevator for getting the coal into the hopper. The internal workings of this plant would be most interesting to see.

(H. H. Harwood, Jr.)

Simplicity itself is this Central Vermont station, which consists of a square box on pillars and a crude elevator of some type. No roof is even supplied on this very simple, small capacity tower.

(TLC Publishing Collection)

Missouri Pacific's timber coaling station at Decatur, Illinois, is the backdrop for this nicely polished Mikado about 1933. The coaling tower appears to have two bins, one for each side, each with a single chute for delivery. All of these towers employ huge timber members for support of the weight of the full coal bins.

(Jay Williams Collection)

Typical Frame Coaling Stations from the Major Builders

The three accompanying illustrations on this page all show typical wooden frame tower type coaling stations available from the major builders. These appeared in the 1929 edition of *Railway Engineering and Maintenance Cyclopedia.* The advertisements that accompanied them in this publication from each of the builders emphasized concrete facilities rather than these frame towers, but apparently they still offered these styles if the customer wanted. The Ogle ad mentioned that it had built over 600 coaling stations for 66 different railroads since it began in this business in 1911 (a period of only 18 years). This gives us some idea as to the quantity of coaling stations built in America, since that figure represented only one of three big builders of this type facility. This tells us two things: first, tower style coaling stations, of one type or another, were virtually everywhere on railroads, and second, they were of relatively modern construction (post-1910 we'll say). It's also evident that the concrete facility had virtually replaced the wooden frame style by this time. Indeed, the earlier, 1921 edition of the *Cyclopedia* also shows a preponderance of concrete and steel facilities with only a couple of frame structures being discussed and illustrated. However, it's equally evident that many railroads had modern wooden frame stations by this time and kept them in service.

C&O Wooden Frame Coaling Station at English Lake, Indiana

We are fortunate to have surviving a set of detailed photos showing the C&O coaling station at English Lake, Indiana, taken in 1939 for use in an accident investigation. The photos show the structure from different angles and vividly illustrate its manner of construction, while hinting at its method of operation. The operation seems to be the usual for bucket conveyor styles with the coal delivered from the incoming hopper car in to a pit, probably with a crusher as in the Thurmond facility illustrated in the drawing on page 11, and then by bucket conveyor to the top of the bins. The interesting feature of this tower is that it has large timbers affixed to the outside of the frame. These certainly give the impression of strengthening the structure. It's not clear if it was built this way or if these are a later modification.

(all C&O Historical Society Collection).

(*above*) Two Big Four (NYC) frame coaling stations show a striking similarity at Van Wert, Ohio (left), and at Riverside Yard, Cincinnati, Ohio (right). Both were photographed in 1921. The Cincinnati facility is obviously the larger in capacity. Van Wert has only one hopper (bin) sloping to the right, whereas Cincinnati has two, with chutes to the right and beneath. Both accepted incoming coal in the shed at left.

(all: Jay Williams Collection,

Tandem coaling stations apparently served NYC's Livernois Yard in this 1939 photo. The one closest to the camera is of frame construction, but immediately back of it can be seen a nearly identical concrete facility.

A large frame facility on the Western Maryland at Cumberland accommodated four large locomotives concurrently. Note the string of hoppers in the left background which apparently loaded coal by means of the skip-jack entering the left side of the corrugated monitor. Photographed in 1948.

(right) North of the border the Canadian Pacific operated this frame coaling station at Ottawa when this photo was made on Aug. 25, 1948. It's a fairly small facility with the major timbers in the frame positioned in X shapes. The usual sand house is very visible on the foreground, and the incoming coal area with an empty hopper under the shed is to the right. Note the discoloration (white) where the stand pipe leads into the frame. Most coaling stations also had sanding facilities attached, with pipes positioned so that the sand could be filled in the same operation as the coaling.

(both: Jay Williams Collection).

A Big Four (NYC) wood frame coal dock at Duane, Indiana (Terre Haute) was equipped to handle locomotives on three tracks, and conforms with other structures from this line shown on previous pages, but is considerably larger.
(Jay Williams Collection)

C&O maintained this interesting small 200-ton wood frame coaling station at Sproul, W. Va., on its Coal River Branch, to replenish locomotives involved in mine shifter work and those headed toward the main line with outbound coal trains. It had a single hopper bin from which chutes extended under the tower and to the track on the outside. No. 2740, one of the line's all-purpose 2-8-4s, is approaching in 1949.
(Gene Huddleston)

Reinforced Concrete Coaling Stations

This section deals with the most common modern coaling station structures, those built from reinforced concrete. They generally follow the designs prevalent in the wooden frame towers, and most use either a conveyor or a skip-hoist system to charge the bins with coal. As locomotives had become more sophisticated the stations occasionally were provided with separate bins for different grades of coal that may have been used by separate classes of locomotives on a single railroad when needed.

Most were built by the previously mentioned major engineering companies: Fairbanks, Morse & Company, the Ogle Engineering Company, and Roberts & Schaefer Company, all with headquarters in America's railroad hub, Chicago. FM offered both skip-hoist and conveyer styles, as did Ogle, but R&S concentrated mainly on the skip-hoist styles. Each company had a variety of standard designs depending on the capacity and type of hoisting being done. Therefore it's easy to see coaling stations among a wide variety of railroads in diverse locations which look very similar.

The concrete coaling stations were either angular in shape with squared corners much as the wood frame designs were, or the main body of the bin was cylindrical in shape. These structures began to be built about 1910, and we believe that the last new construction was at Iaeger, W. Va., on the Norfolk and Western in 1956. By far the bulk were built in the 1920s and 1930s as railroads modernized. By the end of WWII diesels were making major inroads, and few new coaling stations were built. Because of the sturdy nature of these massive structures they were often left in place after the end of steam and continued to be used as supporting structures for sanding facilities or yard lights. Only recently have the ravages of time finally taken their toll, and many railroads began to systematically demolish these last huge remnants of the age of steam, which truly was an age of giants.

In 1923 a transition is occurring in this photo at Atlantic Coast Line's Florence, S.C. yard, as the large multi-track wooden coaling station in the background is being replaced by the much smaller (because it was much more efficient) concrete facility being built in the foreground.

In basic design the concrete coaling station on the C&O at Thurmond, W. Va. is a simple rectangular shape executed in concrete. This photo is looking east on August 5, 1953, toward the end of steam. Both long and short chutes allow coaling of locomotives on either track to the right. Main-line tracks are on the left.

(D. Wallace Johnson)

A C&O H-8 class 2-6-6-6 has just taken on coal at the Thurmond coaling station in September 1955. The arrangement of chutes is exactly the same as on the other side, to accommodate both main lines.

(Gene Huddleston photo, C&O Historical Society collection)

See pages 10-11 for drawings of this facility.

Standard Track Arrangements
for Skip-Hoist Locomotive Coaling Stations

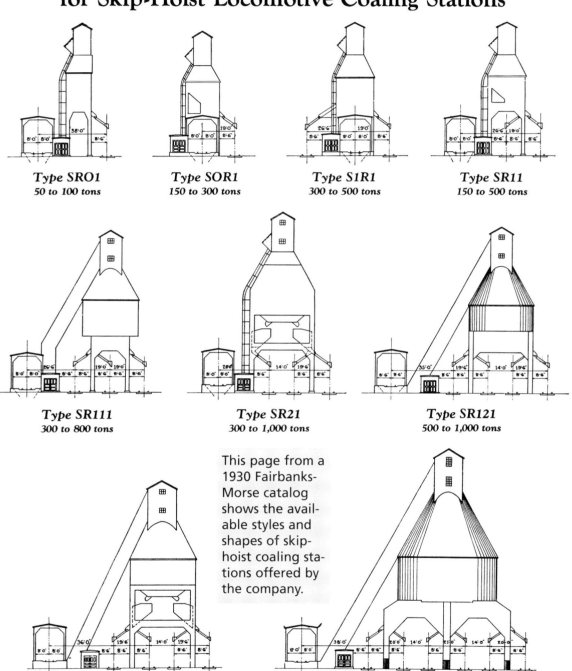

Type SRO1
50 to 100 tons

Type SOR1
150 to 300 tons

Type S1R1
300 to 500 tons

Type SR11
150 to 500 tons

Type SR111
300 to 800 tons

Type SR21
300 to 1,000 tons

Type SR121
500 to 1,000 tons

This page from a 1930 Fairbanks-Morse catalog shows the available styles and shapes of skip-hoist coaling stations offered by the company.

Type SR121
500 to 1,000 tons

Type SR1221
1,000 to 2,000 tons

Other track arrangements and designs are made to suit local conditions

Page Seventeen

Standard Track Arrangements
for Conveyor-Type Locomotive Coaling Stations

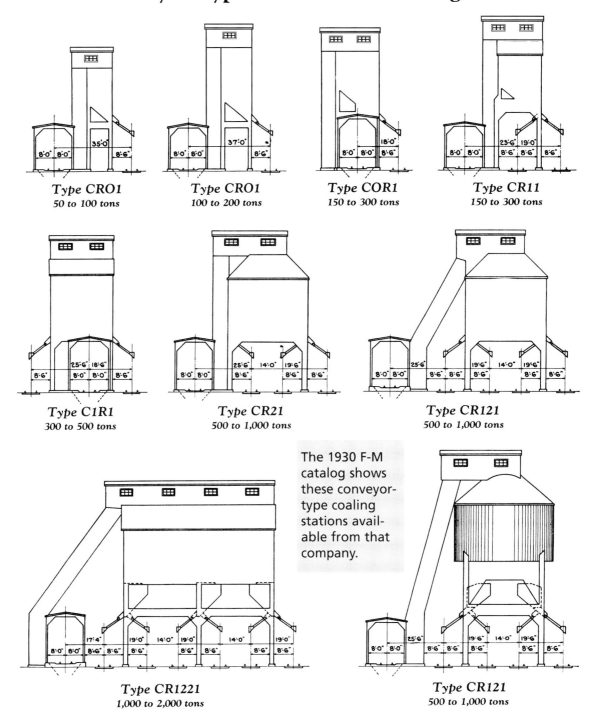

The 1930 F-M catalog shows these conveyor-type coaling stations available from that company.

Type CRO1
50 to 100 tons

Type CRO1
100 to 200 tons

Type COR1
150 to 300 tons

Type CR11
150 to 300 tons

Type C1R1
300 to 500 tons

Type CR21
500 to 1,000 tons

Type CR121
500 to 1,000 tons

Type CR1221
1,000 to 2,000 tons

Type CR121
500 to 1,000 tons

Other track arrangements and designs are made to suit local conditions

Chicago & Northwestern's coaling station at Western Ave. engine terminal, Chicago, accommodated engines on two tracks to the left and one on the right, and its coal seems to be fed up by a conveyor arrangement internal to the structure at the left (where the hopper is spotted). Note that the monitor is located on the left, indicating that's where the conveyor system was. Most coaling stations use an external lift system, making this unusual.

This 1928 photo shows the Atlantic Coast Line coaling station at High Springs, Florida. A simple cylindrical bin with an external skip-hoist facility, it is being used to fuel a passenger train.

An almost identical ACL station at Moncrief, Florida is portrayed in this photo. The legend "ACL 1924" is molded into the concrete at the top.

The C&O bought coaling stations from all three builders. The design shown at left, at Hinton, W. Va., holding 800 tons was almost exactly duplicated at two other major terminals, Richmond, Va., and Stevens, Ky. (serving Cincinnati). Built by Fairbanks-Morse, the design can be compared with their standard designs shown earlier.
(C&O Railway, C&O Historical Society Collection)

This end elevation of the Hinton coaling station, is taken from a rather unclear Fairbanks-Morse drawing used in its construction in 1929. The engineers for some reason attempted to tint the superstructure to make it look like solid concrete, but it just obscures the dimensions.
(C&O Historical Society Collection)

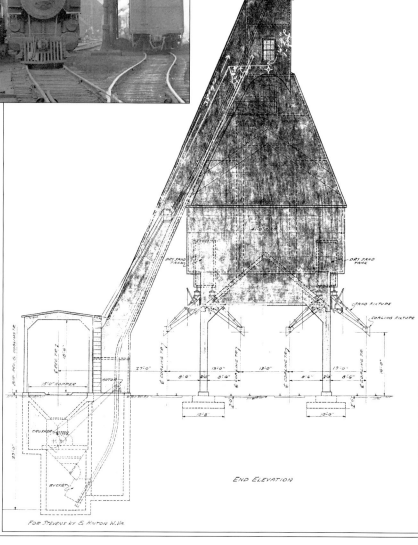

END ELEVATION

FOR STEVENS KY & HINTON W.VA.

-M drawing showing the side elevation of the Hinton, W. Va. C&O coaling station.

Modelers may find these drawings useful, but the scale will have to be determined by using the dimensional markings shown.

Late era photo of the very similar coaling station at C&O's Fulton Yard in Richmond, Va. By this time it has lost its chutes and exterior machinery, but in this 1977 photo was still in active use for sanding diesels and as a tower for yard lights. It has now been demolished.

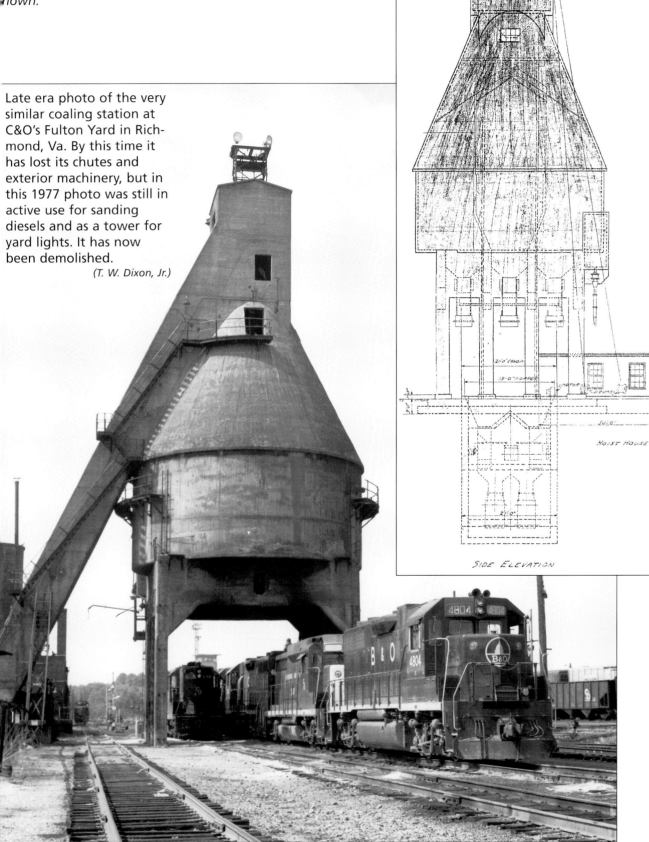

HOIST HOUSE

SIDE ELEVATION

Baltimore & Ohio's major terminal at Garrett, Indiana, had this cylindrical skip-hoist tower with an amazing maze of wires, pulleys, and tracks involved with the hoisting mechanism. It looks like a fairly small station for this important a location, probably 200 tons.

(Jay Williams Collection)

(*right*) The Pennsylvania Railroad had this nicely proportioned station at Bradford Junction, Ohio. It illustrates well how the servicing operations could be closely integrated: note the sand house at the left and the sanding pipes appended to the coaling station, and that the fireman is filling his tender with water even while the coal is still flowing down the chute into the coal bunker. The external skip-hoist apparatus tends to make these facilities less attractive than the enclosed hoists and conveyors.

(Jay Williams Collection)

(*right*) Small cylindrical coaling stations tended to be squat, with capacity increased by increasing the diameter of the cylinder bin, but in the case of this Nickel Plate Road coal dock at Conneaut, Ohio, it's fairly large 700-ton capacity was accommodated by elongating the cylinder. This facility was built in 1924 and was the first modern concrete NKP coaling station.

(Paul Prescott, John B. Corns Collection)

No. 1211, one of Norfolk and Western's A-Class simple articulated 2-6-6-4s, is stopped under the coaling station at Columbus, Ohio on November , 1957. This facility has an extraordinary number of catwalks and steel details as well as the anding drums positioned on stanchions nearby, ll giving the location a nice feel of compact ctivity. Note that immediately to the right ackground is a cinder conveyor and a hopper or receiving the ashes. Later in this book the inder conveyors will be treated. It was always a ood guess that very near the coaling station vas an ash pit. In this case it seems to be in a traight line with the coaling station tracks. Note also that beneath the tower the coal hutes drop straight down rather than being eflected through aprons and inclined chutes. his must have allowed a faster flow of the oal, but must also have required a very differnt cut-off and regulating system.

(Steve Patterson)

he Boston & Albany coaling station at oston was one of the larger of the cylindrial style. It's unusual in that it has a two-rack unloading pit, so that two hoppers can e unloaded into the conveyor at once, indiating the huge capacity inherent in this size tation. The concrete silo in the right backround is the sand house.

(Jay Williams Collection)

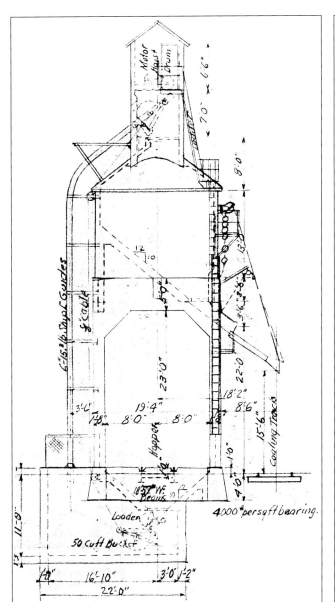

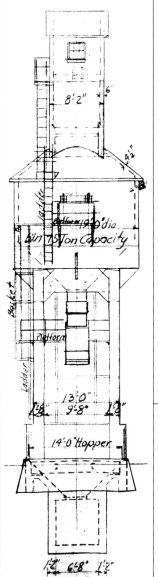

The drawings and photograph on this page show C&O's 75-ton concrete coaling station at Ronceverte, W. Va., a small main-line yard with responsibility mainly for local business and as terminal for a 100-mile branch line into logging country. It was erected by Ogle in 1935, and is still standing in almost complete condition as of this writing in 2002. Coal was loaded from the center, and there was one delivery chute on the left. Modelers will find this particularly interesting because it looks like big coaling stations, but is very small in size. In 1999 Walthers Models produced a plastic kit that very closely approximates this design.

(All, C&O Historical Society collection)

Baltimore & Ohio's coaling station at Fairmont, W. Va. represents a hybrid design that has its bin in a cylinder, but the rest of the mechanism combined into an encased conveyer, monitor, and machinery housing. Built about 1930, it served the Fairmont yard which was a marshalling point in the B&O's northern West Virginia coal fields. Photo at left was taken in 1930, and the one above in 1946.
(both, Jay Williams Collection)

Another interesting B&O design is at Akron Junction, Ohio. It is loaded by a hopper run up a ramp and dumped to a conveyer house located on the ground rather than in a pit. This may have been to facilitate maintenance. It also has a very long, twisted delivery chute, supported at the end by steel girders. It appears to be no larger than 75-tons in capacity.

(John Rehor photo)

Coaling stations were sometimes built away from terminals at relatively isolated locations on the main line because of the need to refuel locomotives on heavy grades or in long operating territories. This photo shows the Norfolk and Western facility at Farm, W. Va. in August 1954. Note that this location also had two large water tanks. Water stations were more likely to be seen away from terminals than were coaling stations.

(D. Wallace Johnson)

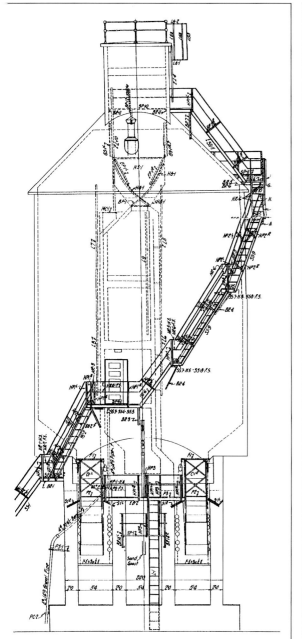

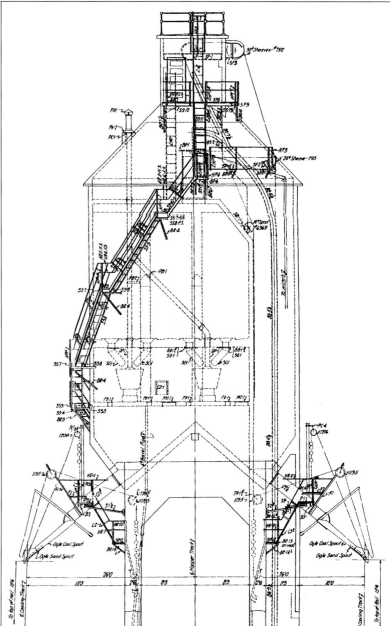

The drawings on this page show the Ogle 300-ton coaling station on the C&O's James River Subdivision at Balcony Falls, Va. Built in 1942, it replaced a wooden structure that dated from the turn of the 20th Century. The main purpose of the facility was to refuel coal trains between Clifton Forge and Richmond, Va. while stopped on the main line. It fits the non-terminal type operation. On the following page is an illustration of Balcony Falls as well as a similar facility at West Hamlin, W. Va.

(all, C&O Historical Society Collection)

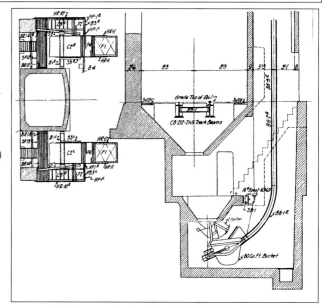

Two very similar Ogle coaling stations built for C&O. At the left is the Balcony Falls facility (taken in 1978 with most of its equipment intact (see previous page for drawings), and on the right is a nearly identical facility on the C&O's Logan branch in the southern West Virginia coal fields at West Hamlin. This facility also fueled engines on trains stopped on the main line. The only noticeable difference is that Balcony Falls delivers coal on both sides, and W. Hamlin on one side and in the center with a loading pit on the other side. Balcony Falls loads from the center.

(both, C&O Historical Society Collection)

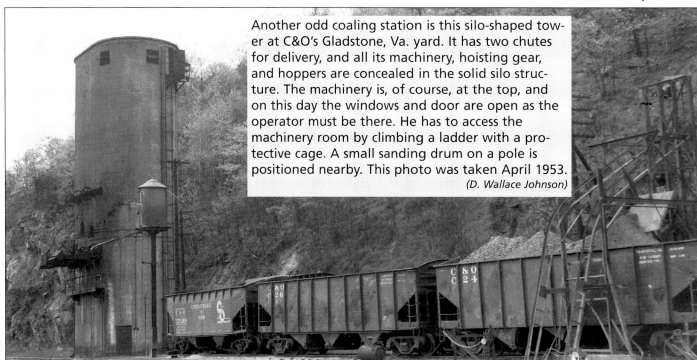

Another odd coaling station is this silo-shaped tower at C&O's Gladstone, Va. yard. It has two chutes for delivery, and all its machinery, hoisting gear, and hoppers are concealed in the solid silo structure. The machinery is, of course, at the top, and on this day the windows and door are open as the operator must be there. He has to access the machinery room by climbing a ladder with a protective cage. A small sanding drum on a pole is positioned nearby. This photo was taken April 1953.

(D. Wallace Johnson)

Occasionally coaling stations were built so that they had separate storage bins on both sides of the tracks. This was usually the case when it was necessary to fuel locomotives standing on several tracks at once, most often on the main line. The usual accommodation for fueling multiple tracks was to add extended chutes on both sides and even under the tower. However, some railroads apparently specified the separate bins for one reason or another. In the cases when this design was employed, a single set of hoisting machinery and engine was used to deliver coal into both bunkers. At left is the Nickel Plate Road facility at East 75th Street, Cleveland, Ohio, photographed in March 1949 with a westbound manifest freight passing beneath. The monitor with the machinery is positioned high above the two bins. Hopper cars delivering coal to the station were positioned under the right tower, and the coal was hoisted up the center apparently using a bucket mechanism.

(Jay Williams Collection)

The Illinois Central used this very large double coaling station at Dawson Springs, Kentucky. As can be seen, the coal arrived under the left tower and was conveyed, probably by steel bucket conveyor, to the machinery house, then sent via flat conveyor to the opposite tower, when needed. This is also an example of what I am calling a "mainline" facility, used to fuel locomotives en route rather than at terminals. At any rate, it's an impressive structure. This seems to be a builder's photo, but there is no identification as to the builder.

This 1947 photo shows B&O's mainline coaling station near Warwick, Oh. as a large example with the towers on each side of the track. The two large hoppers straddle the main lines, with the delivery chutes located under the structure. As usual with these dual-tower structures, the monitor and conveyor system is located a good deal higher than the bins. In this case, incoming coal is delivered between the two towers (note row of empty hopper cars).

(Jay Williams Collection)

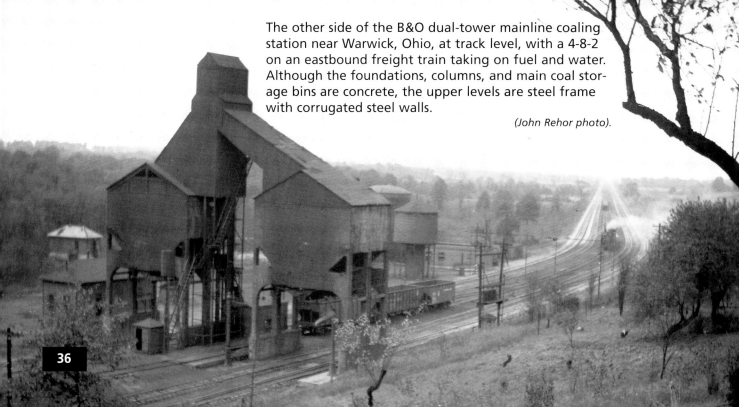

The other side of the B&O dual-tower mainline coaling station near Warwick, Ohio, at track level, with a 4-8-2 on an eastbound freight train taking on fuel and water. Although the foundations, columns, and main coal storage bins are concrete, the upper levels are steel frame with corrugated steel walls.

(John Rehor photo).

Built on a design roughly the same as the drawing below, the NYC coaling station at Collinwood, Ohio (Cleveland) is seen in this 1945 photo. The major difference with the top drawing is that its hoisting equipment in encased.
(Jay Williams Collection)

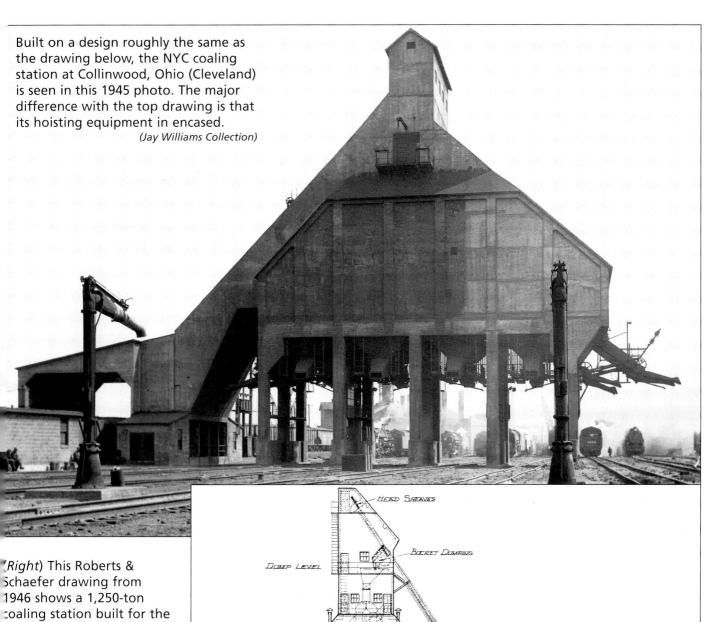

(*Right*) This Roberts & Schaefer drawing from 1946 shows a 1,250-ton coaling station built for the Pennsylvania Railroad. It accommodates chutes on six tracks, has an integral sand bin and dryer, and receives coal from a double track unloading pit, the coal being conveyed to the storage bins by means of skip hoist buckets. The hoisting motor is located on the ground next to the unloading pits. This shape was apparently common for larger coaling stations that had to fuel numerous locomotives at once. Using 50-ton hopper cars, it would take a train of 25 cars just to fill this coaling station once!

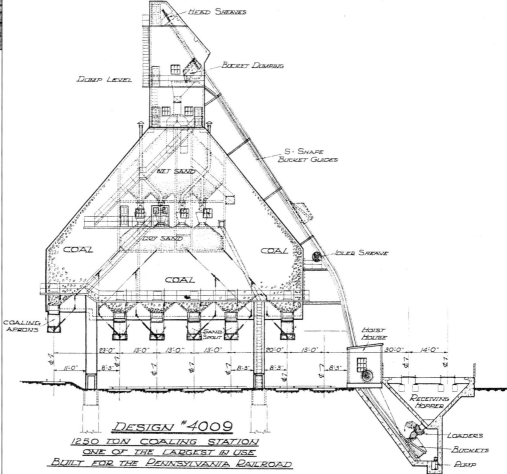

HEAD SHEAVES

BUCKET DUMPING

DUMP LEVEL

S-SHAPE BUCKET GUIDES

WET SAND

COAL

COAL

DRY SAND

IDLER SHEAVE

COAL

COALING APRONS

SAND SPOUT

HOIST HOUSE

23'-0" 13'-0" 13'-0" 13'-0" 20'-0" 13'-0" 30'-0" 14'-0"

11'-0" 8'-3" 8'-3" 8'-3"

RECEIVING HOPPER

LOADERS

BUCKETS

PUMP

DESIGN #4009
1250 TON COALING STATION
ONE OF THE LARGEST IN USE
BUILT FOR THE PENNSYLVANIA RAILROAD

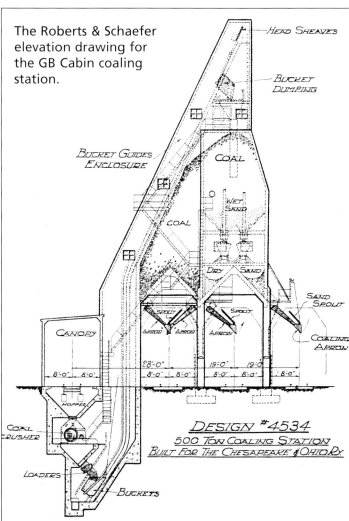

The Roberts & Schaefer elevation drawing for the GB Cabin coaling station.

HEAD SHEAVES

BUCKET DUMPING

BUCKET GUIDES ENCLOSURE

COAL

WET SAND

COAL

DRY SAND

SAND SPOUT

CANOPY

SPOUT

APRON APRON

APRON

SPOUT

COALING APRON

HOPPER

COAL CRUSHER

LOADERS

BUCKETS

DESIGN #4534
500 TON COALING STATION
BUILT FOR THE CHESAPEAKE & OHIO RY

The C&O's mainline coaling station at GB Cabin, Oh., was built by Roberts & Schaefer in 1946 and was of the most modern semi-streamlined design. With almost all its machinery encased in concrete, it presented a very smooth appearance. Otherwise of standard function and design, the facility served until diesels supplanted the giant 2-6-6-6s seen in the photos in 1952.

(Gene Huddleston)

In November 1950 an empty coal train leaves the GB Cabin coaling station.
(Gene Huddleston)

The B&O Coaling Station at Sir John's Run, W. Va. was of the rectangular (or almost square in this case) design, with two hoppers and coaling aprons for four tracks. The hoist is straight, with the buckets dumping down an inclined chute into storage bins. This differs from the majority of hoisting arrangements. More usually the skip hoist or conveyor buckets go to a dumping location near the center of the bin arrangement.

(Jay Williams Collection).

The Nickel Plate coal dock at Pomfort, N. Y. (seen here in Sept. 1946), has an arrangement very similar to the B&O Sir Johns Run facility. Coaling was done under the tower.

(Jay Williams Collection)

The Pennsylvania Railroad coaling station at Marion, Oh., is shown here in its twilight on April 20, 1957, with J-1a 2-10-4 No. 6169 taking on water. This very symmetrical style with the external skip hoist was seen at many PRR locations. The distinctive pilasters on the bin differentiate it from the smooth-sided coal bin structures on many other railroads.

(John Rehor, Jay Williams Collection)

C&O's Shelby, Ky. 300-ton coaling station was built by Fairbanks-Morse in 1918, and in service to the end of steam.

(Photo by D. Wallace Johnson in 1952).

Drawings are from original F-M erection drawings.

(C&OHS Collection)

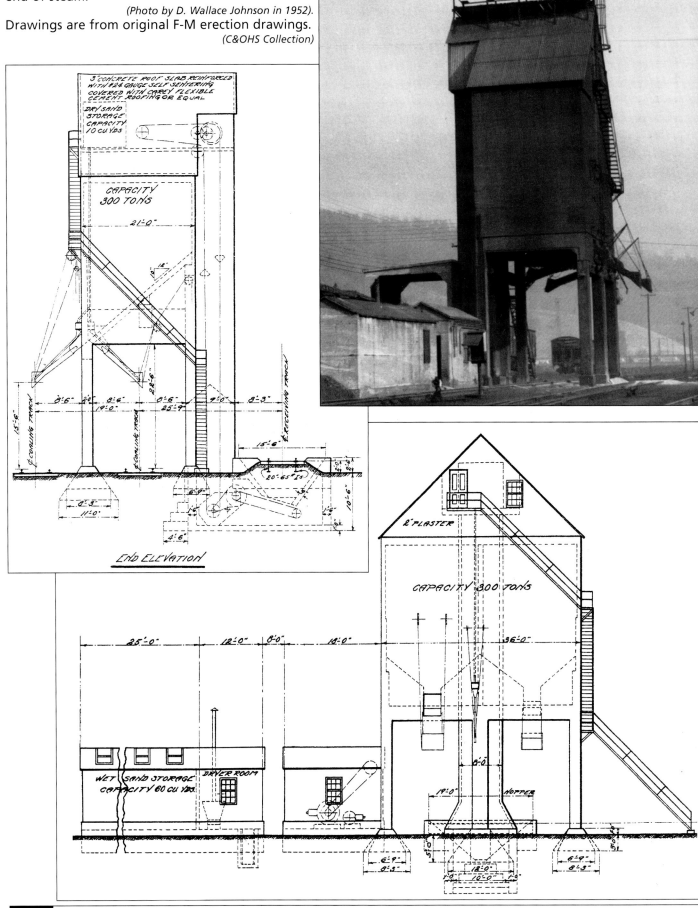

Another view of the Shelby, Ky. coaling station, with a locomotive taking fuel and sand. Modelers will note that this very old tower is well-blackened with soot from the many locomotives that have stood under it over the years. The facility was built in 1918 and is shown near the end of its life in 1952.

(D. Wallace Johnson photo)

A classic coaling station scene at the Nickel Plate's Bellevue, Ohio engine terminal. The 500-ton coaling station (built 1925) looms in the background as NKP's famous Berkshire 2-8-4s congregate. The coaling station itself has a rather high peaked roof and the dumping machinery isn't encased in concrete. Photo was taken in Sept. 1946.

(John B. Corns Collection)

41

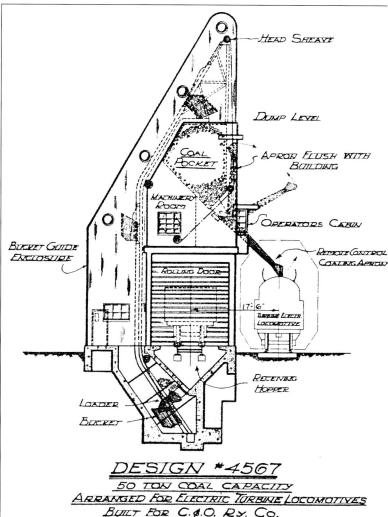

DESIGN #4567
50 TON COAL CAPACITY
ARRANGED FOR ELECTRIC TURBINE LOCOMOTIVES
BUILT FOR C.&O. RY. CO.

One of the most unusual and most specialized coaling stations ever built was this "streamlined" C&O facility. The design was intended to compliment the huge streamlined steam-turbine-electric (STE) locomotives that Baldwin/GE built for C&O's projected new ultra-luxurious all-coach Washington-Cincinnati daylight *Chessie* streamliner. C&O, the world's largest originator of bituminous coal, tried to keep coal alive as a railroad fuel by developing the STE. One of these streamlined coaling stations was located at the west end of the passenger platform at Clifton Forge, Va., and another at the east end of the platform at Hinton, W. Va. When the Turbines pulled up for a station stop, they were coaled as the passengers were boarding and detraining. The train was cancelled and the turbines spent only a year in service before being scrapped. As can be seen from the Roberts & Schaefer drawing, the facility held only 50 tons of coal, since that was all that would be needed to fuel one turbine once daily. Painted silver and yellow, with a stylized C&O herald on it, this was the realization of the streamline idiom on the most pedestrian of railroad machinery.

(All C&O Ry, C&O Hist. Soc. Collection)

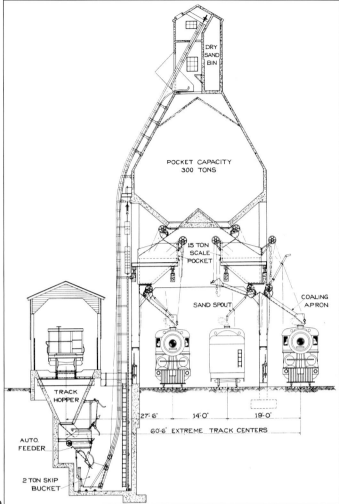

The photo and drawing are from the 1930 edition of the Fairbanks-Morse coaling station catalog. They illustrate the measured and counter-balanced bucket style. In this relatively rare type, the coal was dumped from the main bin into a bucket, where it was weighed and then dumped, bucket at a time, into engine tenders through ordinary coaling chutes and aprons. The photo F-M used to illustrate this design was built for the Santa Fe at Lamy, N. M.

This illustration from the June, 1915 *Railway Age Gazette, Mechanical Edition*, shows an L&N coaling station with usual bucket delivery system from cars to the bin. The difference was that it also provided for ground storage, so that coal could be piled up by a crane and then delivered to the coaling station as needed, rather than relying only on direct delivery from cars. This was not adopted very widely because of the large space needed.

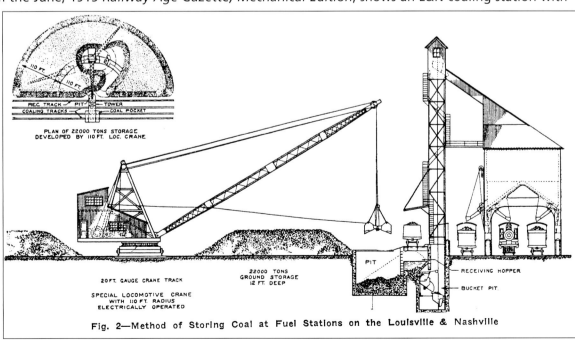

Fig. 2—Method of Storing Coal at Fuel Stations on the Louisville & Nashville

Canadian railroads used coaling stations of basically the same designs and styles as their U.S. counterparts. Illustrated here is the Canadian National coaling station at Spadina engine terminal in Toronto (taken in 1980, still in use for sanding diesels). Only the coaling chutes and aprons have been removed. It employed three separate bins, supplied by a conveyor at the top, and could accommodate simultaneous coaling of four locomotives.
(Kevin J. Holland photo)

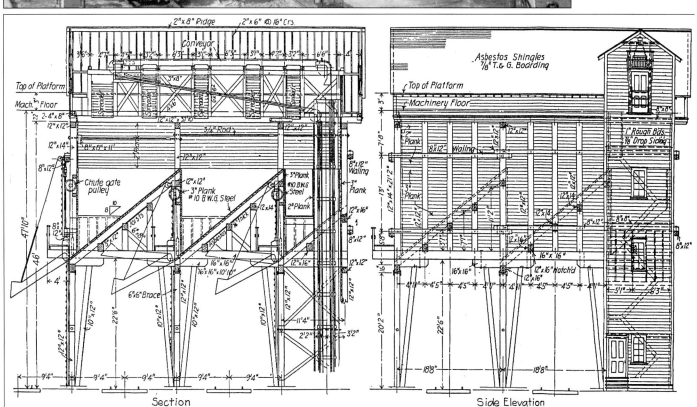

Section

Side Elevation

This drawing appeared in the November 15, 1924 edition of *Railway Review* and depicts the Canadian National's then new three-hopper (or bin) wood frame coaling station at Moncton, New Brunswick. It used a bucket-conveyor to elevate the coal and then a flat conveyor belt to place it in each of the bins.

The Norfolk & Western Railway's huge 2,000-ton coaling station at Bluefield, W. Va. was built by Ogle between June, 1951 and December 1952, at a cost to the company of $400,000. At the time of its construction it was the largest facility of the type in the world, when the capacity for sand (200 tons) and slack coal for boiler house use (another 150 tons) were considered. It was in service until the last N&W steam was withdrawn in 1959. It is often considered the last coaling station built, but N&W built yet one more, a relatively small 200-ton tower at Iaeger, W. Va., in 1956.

The cylindrical storage bin area was 32-feet in diameter with side wall thickness of 10-inches of reinforced concrete, and the outside was covered with an anti-weathering compound with an appearance of tar.

The conveyor system, which consisted of two 1-1/2-ton skip hoist buckets, was arranged vertically because of congested yard conditions around the structure. The buckets could deliver 300-tons of coal per hour to the hoppers (bins) within the tower. At the top, incoming coal was passed over an Orienz magnetic separator to remove any iron or steel objects that might contaminate the coal (and thus cause problems with locomotive stokers). From there it went directly to the bins, to a crusher for re-sizing, or a screen. The screen removed slack, which was placed in the bin for use in the nearby boiler house. Since the climate in Bluefield is cold in the winter and freezing of coal load occurred, heaters and shakers were provided at the unloading tracks. The facility still stands at this writing (2002) in the Norfolk Southern yard, a reminder of the N&W's last years of steam.

The upper photo is an N&W publicity shot, with two of the road's famous high-efficiency locomotives, a Class A and Class Y-6, taking on fuel. The lower photo shows the tower partially complete, during the construction phase, taken by Roger F. Whitt.

(courtesy N&W Historical Society)

In full service in 1953, the Bluefield coaling station is seen from across the yard, clearly showing the wide concrete casing over the bucket hoisting system. Some maintenance problems were caused by its being enclosed in this casing, since its parts weren't as accessible as in the open style.
(Roger Whitt, courtesy N&W Historical Society)

Photos and data about the Bluefield coaling station were condensed, with permission, from an article by James Gillum in the N&W Historical Society's Magazine, *The Arrow*.

This July 1957 photo shows another interesting N&W coaling facility: Portsmouth, Oh. It also had a 2,000-ton capacity in two bins. This was similar to the Bluefield facility except it had its hoisting machinery on an incline and it was exposed rather than cased. With top the dumping area in the open, automatically opening and closing steel hatches activated by the arriving buckets of coal kept the weather out of the bins. As with Bluefield, the track pit covered two tracks, so that two lines of cars could be dumped concurrently. Each of the two hoisting mechanisms could elevate 75 tons of coal per hour for a combined capacity of 150 tons. Unlike most stations, the space under the conical roof was used for coal storage as well as the cylinder. The cylinder body was 55 feet in diameter. The entire structure stood 135 feet high. Six locomotives could be served at once.

(Joe Schmitz photo)

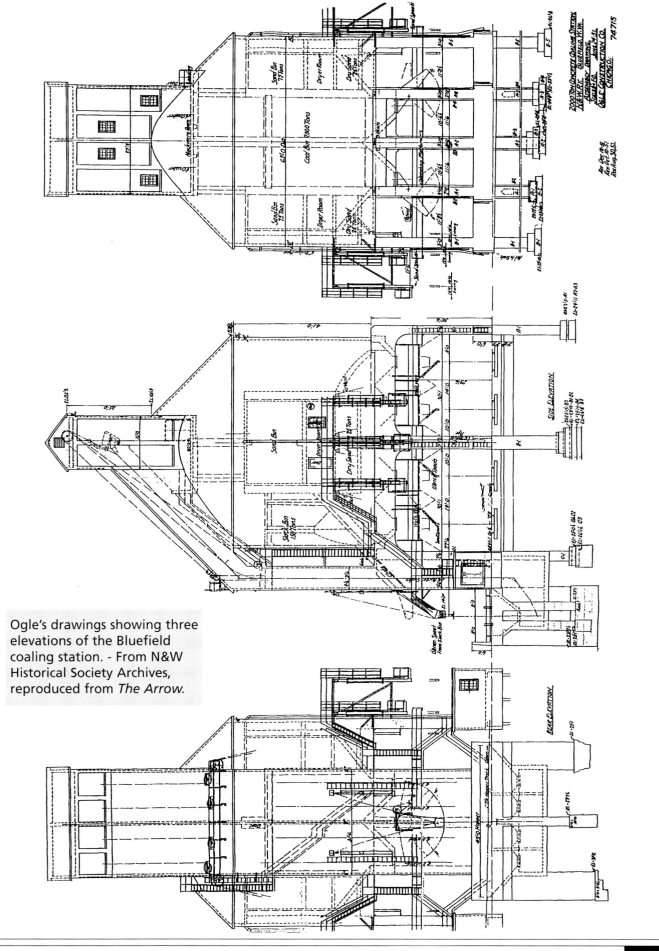

Ogle's drawings showing three elevations of the Bluefield coaling station. - From N&W Historical Society Archives, reproduced from *The Arrow*.

The drawings and photo on this page illustrate the 1,000-ton coaling station at Russell, Ky., on the Chesapeake & Ohio. Built in 1925 by Ogle, it was the largest on the entire C&O system. The other major terminals had 800 or 500-ton stations. Russell was the C&O's most active engine terminal and largest yard, thus the need to have storage capacity sufficient so that the bin would not have to be recharged so frequently. However, compared with N&W, its coal hauling neighbor, C&O's coaling facilities were smallish.

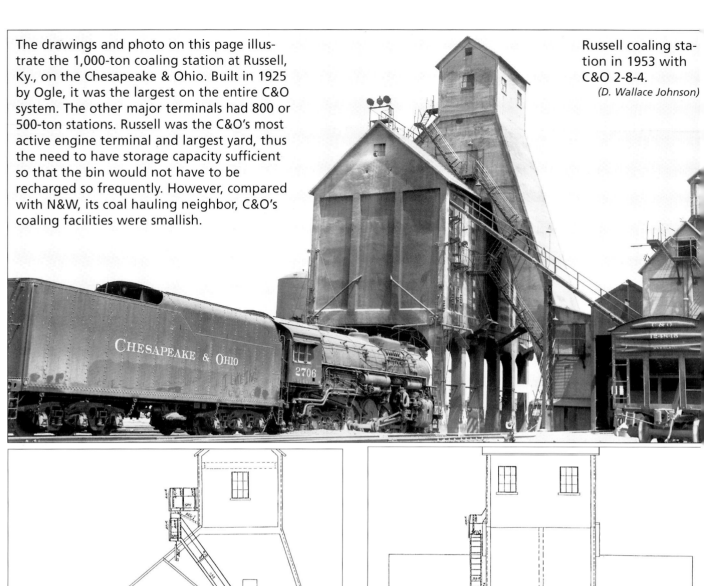

Russell coaling station in 1953 with C&O 2-8-4.

(D. Wallace Johnson)

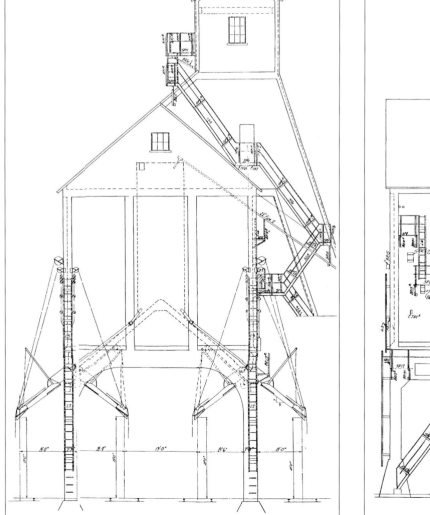

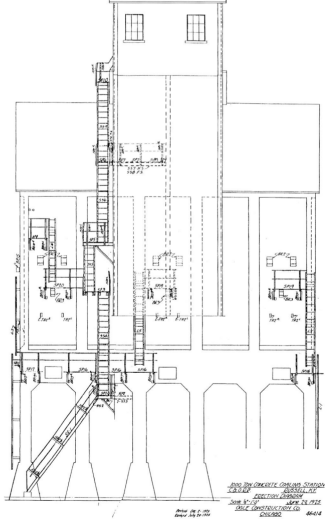

At about the same time as the introduction of concrete as a replacement material for wood in coaling stations, some of the new mechanical types begin to be built from steel. These continued to be used and built during the same time period as the concrete stations up to the end of steam, but they are far fewer in number and generally were used in locations where a very limited space was available and for relatively small capacities. The inherent difficulty of maintenance and weathering of the steel structures were their major disadvantages. All three of the major builders erected steel towers, as well as some smaller construction companies, while a few were designed by railroad company engineers in house.

The four photos above are taken from the 1929 edition of *Railway Engineering & Maintenance Cyclopedia* (page 631), and represent typical steel coaling stations then being advertised by the three major builders. As can be seen, they are all different in shape, design, and particular features, and range in bin capacity from small to medium. The Fairbanks, Morse design even employs a concrete-encased hoisting system attached to the steel bin and delivery equipment. Both Roberts & Schaefer designs use an angular shaped bin instead of the cylinder.

(*left*) The photo at left, also taken from the 1929 edition of *Railway Engineering & Maintenance Cyclopedia*, illustrates a steel coaling station erected by the Howlett Construction Co. of Moline, Illinois. The company's ad copy emphasized the patented hoisting motors and self-loading bucket and loaders. Howelett's ad stated that it had been in the business of building coaling stations of wood, concrete and steel for 15 years.

(*above, left & right*) The Nickel Plate had a number of steel coaling stations as shown on the two photos above. The facility on the left was at Yukon, Illinois (photographed 1954). The photo on the right shows the facility at Muncie, Indiana in 1944. The two are nearly identical in construction. We don't know the capacity of the bin but it was probably about 100-tons or perhaps less. The shed over the unloading pit track is wooden!

(*left Paul Stringham, Jay Williams Collection - right John Rehor photo*)

A third, nearly identical facility is depicted here at Charleston, Illinois.

(*Richard Cook photo*)

(*below, center and left*) In the 1930s railroads began to plan engine servicing facilities with an eye to increased efficiency and quicker turn-around. This included consolidating as much of the operation as possible in one place. The coaling station, usually the largest facility involved, was the natural center. The two photos above depict a "one-stop"

coaling station that has an ash pit directly below it, water columns, and sanding pipes, so that a locomotive can have its fire cleaned and ashes dumped while taking on coal, water, and sand. Usually, only the coal and sanding operations were located. This station, with its unusual steel bins positioned at right angles, was installed in 1941 on the Lehigh Valley at Towanda, N. Y. It was a "mainline" facility refueling locomotives *en route* from Buffalo to Jersey City, allowing one engine to cover the 450 miles without change. The station was built by Roberts & Schaefer.

(*top right*) Akron, Canton & Youngstown's tower (left) is spiderlike in appearance, while the Duluth, Missabe & Iron Range facility (*above left*) seems incongruously small to be filling the huge 2-8-8-4's tender. Both are steel structures.

(*right*) This New York Central all-steel design has a large capacity, gained by incorporating two conical-bottom steel cylinder bins with the usual conveyor arrangement for dumping coal in either.

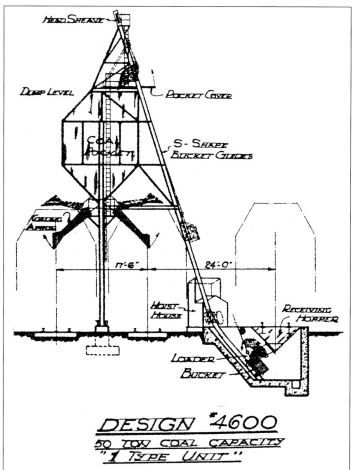

DESIGN #4600
50 TON COAL CAPACITY
"1 TYPE UNIT"

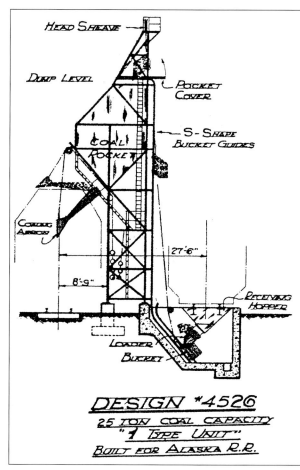

DESIGN #4526
25 TON COAL CAPACITY
"1 TYPE UNIT"
BUILT FOR ALASKA R.R.

(*above & right*) Three Roberts & Schaefer steel coaling station designs from a 1946 brochure show two 50-ton and one tiny 25-ton capacity stations. The 25-ton tower is the smallest capacity facility in any materials we have located. Generally, anything less would be better accommodated by an "automatic coaler," which will be treated later in this book.

(*above*) Grand Trunk's "mainline" steel coaling station near South Bend, Indiana, is coaling a passenger special in 1956. Note several hopper cars of coal on the siding at left, ready to be loaded as needed.

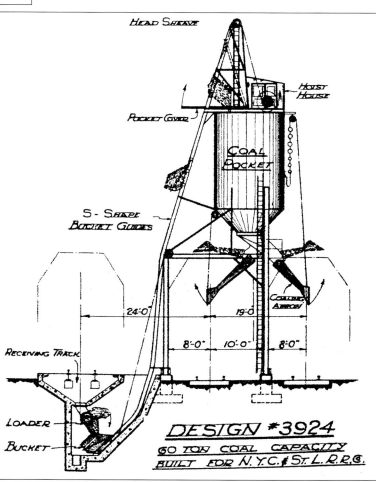

DESIGN #3924
60 TON COAL CAPACITY
BUILT FOR N.Y.C. & St. L. R.R.

Although most coaling stations constructed of structural steel were small in capacity, a few were quite large. The photo above shows the Union Pacific coaling station at Green River, Wyoming, about 1956, still with plenty of locomotives to service. The station was built in much the same style as a rectangular concrete one, with the shed for receiving incoming coal cars on the right and an inclined conveyor system elevating the coal to the monitor on top where it could be delivered to several bins below.

(Bob Hale photo, Jay Williams Collection)

(above) UP had another large steel facility at Laramie, Wyoming, as shown here. Its sides seem to be large solid plate girders rather than the trussed design seen on the previous page. The trussed bridge in front of the structure isn't attached. It supports two (hard to see) cylindrical hoppers for sand.
(Robert Hale photo, Jay Williams Collection)

(above) Another view of the UP facility at Cheyenne (see previous page) shows coal being delivered to a Challenger. Note that the chute has a canvas skirt which kept down dust and also helped better direct the flow of coal.

(Jay Williams Collection)

(right) A view from beneath the Green River coaling station shows a water column positioned right under the tower. Note also that the coal drops down directly through the canvas-skirted chutes from the hoppers above.

(Bob Hale photo, Jay Williams Collection)

New York Central's Wayneport, N.Y. coaling station was similar to the UP facilities on the previous pages except that it's covered entirely in corrugated steel siding. It also has a girder bridge over the track adjacent to the tower, with two sand hoppers. Capacity must have been large for these towers. These designs weren't in the standard advertisements, catalogues, and promotional materials from the big three builders.

(Jay Williams Collection)

(*above*) A wonderful 1946 photo shows the NYC's big Wayneport, N. Y. coaling station astride the main line. To the left is the old wooden wharf style coaling station that had been kept in use for some purpose. In the 1940s this station serviced 17 westbound and 18 eastbound NYC passenger trains between 9:15 pm and 3:30 am. What a busy place this was, and a testament to the mechanical capacity of the facility.

(Jay Williams Collection)

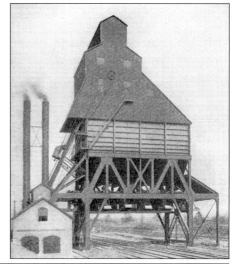

(*right*) This small photo, lifted from *Railway Age* in 1912, shows an 1,800-ton capacity steel girder coaling station on the LS&MS (NYC) at Wesleyville, Pa. It was built by the line's engineering department and the Link Belt Company of Chicago. This is an example of a large capacity steel structure built to a design similar to the concrete stations of the era.

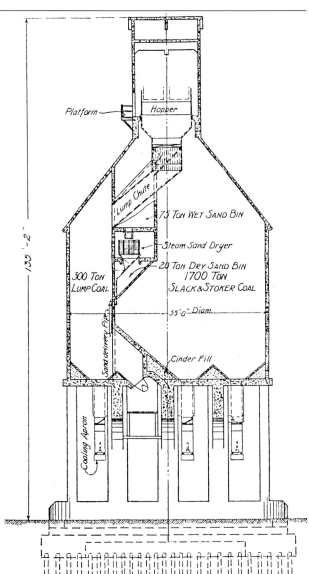

The N&W's huge 2,000-ton coaling station at Prichard, W. Va. (located midway between two major terminals at Williamson, W. Va. and Portsmouth, Ohio), was erected by Roberts & Schaefer in 1926. Screens could separate run-of-mine coal into two grades, one for hand fired engines and one for stokers. A storage yard held coal cars for the station. Cars were moved by gravity to the unloading pits, where 3-ton buckets hoisted the coal to the storage bin.

The photos show the station under construction. It was built to fuel on 6 tracks at once. Visible to the right in the lower photo are the sanding tower and water tower under construction. The Prichard facility offered complete *en route* engine servicing. The train arrived, the locomotive was cut off, taken to the water station, then sanded and finally coaled and returned to the train to resume its run.

(photos and drawings from Railway Review, March 20, 1926)

Automatic Coaling Stations

This designation came to be applied to conveyor systems, either fixed, semi-mobile, or mobile, that were used to deliver coal directly from a pile or from a car to the locomotive tender without storing it in a bin or hopper. They were very simple in concept, inexpensive to build and maintain, and occupied very little space. However, compared with delivery from an elevated bin, the process of coaling was much slower, confined to the capacity of the buckets or conveyor used rather than to gravity flow from a large reservoir through a fairly large gate, as in the standard coaling stations.

This 1920s photograph of the C&O's Elk Yard engine terminal area in Charleston, W. Va. illustrates why the simple automatic coalers were preferred. The space available is about as cramped as possible, with the coaler, ash pit and ash handler, and water station all crammed in next to a bridge. The automatic coaler shown here is a standard of Fairbanks-Morse, and though we have only imperfect photos of it, we have a very good drawing, which is reproduced on page 58.
(C&O Historical Society Collection)

An overhead view of the tiny Elk yard terminal area showing the top of the F-M automatic coaler. A high-sided gondola of coal is positioned over the coaler's pit. Apparently the coal was shoveled through the clearing doors into the pit.
A car of sand is position nearby, and two small locomotives are standing by to be served.
(C&O Historical Society Collection)

See next page for additional material on Elk yard.

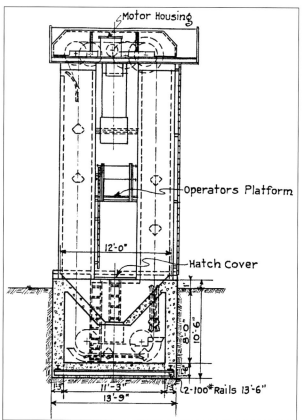

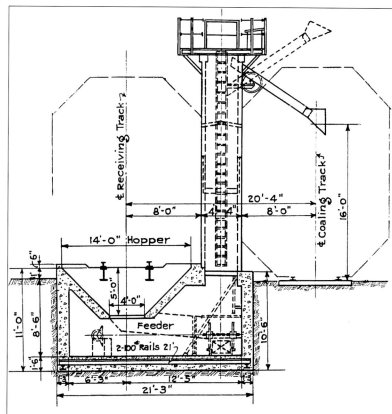

(above) The C&O engineering department drawings show the side and end elevations of the Fairbanks-Morse automatic coaler for Elk yard as it was built. Notes on the drawing indicate that work began June 23, 1930, and was completed October 1, 1930. At least one HO model has been made of this in the 1990s using this drawing and the accompanying photos as source materials.

(below) At another location a Fairbanks-Morse automatic coaler is seen in this very obstructed view. Nonetheless, we can determine most of its appearance from this and the two illustrations on the previous page.

(right) This locally-built coaling station was located at the Interstate Railroad's yard at its Andover, Va. yard in this 1930 photo. The coal was dispensed from the hopper car above into a bucket which traveled up the skip hoist and dumped it directly into the locomotive tender.

N & W TYPE ENGINE COALER

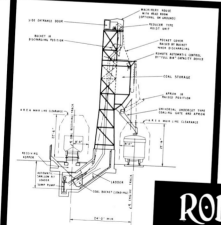

A design "dictated by the job"—this new, up-to-the-minute N & W Type Engine Coaler. Every detail of it *fits* actual working conditions—a design evolved out of long, continuous, first-hand study of the kind of equipment railroads need for dependable, trouble-free economical service—its simplicity keeps maintenance costs low.

Like the Cinder Plants, the engine coaler is of unit construction—assembled and welded in the shop, fully equipped with machinery, delivered complete and ready for erection.

- **Foundation**—Shallow depth of pit with headroom for maintenance.
- **Track Centers** — $22\frac{1}{2}$ ft. minimum with 8 ft. side clearance for engine track, $7\frac{1}{2}$ ft. side clearance for coal car track.
- **Hopper**—Integral part of pit is of reinforced concrete, equipped with track girders and rail bolts, in any required size (10 ft. minimum).
- **Tower**—Rigid frame construction; main members $\frac{5}{16}''$—bucket guides $\frac{3}{8}''$ minimum thickness.
- **Apron**—Coal is discharged into apron with front deflector plate lowered and raised by special ball bearing equipped chain hoist.
- **Machinery House**—On top of tower, full protection of machinery and control switches at all times—no hinged top lid covers. Optional: Machinery house on ground.
- **Bucket**—Shallow pit type of heavy rigid construction —50 cubic foot capacity unrestricted on top to receive ROM coal.
- **Automatic Loaders**—Inclined sliding gate, undercut type, completely guided. A simple arrangement of counterweight, combined with coal pressure, keeps gate positively closed. No springs, cams, latches or triggers. Depression in guides engages or disengages gate for automatic operation by coal hoist bucket. Gravity banking action prevents double charging of bucket even if it is accidentally returned loaded. Ample size to operate with ROM coal.
- **Hoist Unit**—Reducer with standard electric motor (no gear motor). One set of spur gear and pinion for slow speed transmission to drum. Drum machine scored, high test cast iron, cable sheaves of large diameter. Hoisting cables extra flexible, pre-formed.
- **Electric Control**—Full automatic.
- **Capacities**—50 tons per hour with 10 H. P. motor.
  65 tons per hour with 15 H. P. motor.
  90 tons per hour with 20 H. P. motor.
- **Conversion**—N & W type engine coaler can be furnished of straight tower design with storage bin (15 tons or more capacity) with electrically interlocked control starting hoist operation as soon as coal is withdrawn from storage bins.

This page is taken from a Roberts & Schaefer brochure on cinder conveyors and automatic coalers. The exact origin of the name "N&W Type," isn't clear. Note that in the last paragraph the company says that this can supplied with a straight tower with a storage bin at the top (the hoisting mechanism being activated to replenish the bin automatically when coal was withdrawn).

(C&O Historical Society Collection)

The Virginian Railway liked the Roberts & Schaefer automatic coaler and used it in several locations. This photo shows the compact engine facility at Victoria, Virginia, in 1953. The AG class 2-6-6-6 is coming up to the coaler to be serviced. The hoisting bucket is at the top of the tower in the horizontal position where it dumps the coal onto the chute and apron for delivery to the tender.

A water column and sanding tank are nearby to facilitate easy handling of several functions. On the other side of the hoppers is one of the R&S "N&W Type" cinder conveyors actually dumping cinders into one of the cars

(All: H. Reid photo

(*right*) Virginian Railway's terminal at Sewell's Point (Norfolk), Virginia also had Roberts & Schaefer automatic coalers and cinder plants. Here an MB Class 2-8-2 is taking on coal in 1947. The Virginian used the straight tower design. (above) Another view, in 1948, of the Virginian's Sewell's Point engine terminal with the coaling station ready for action. Note the cinder plant in the background, and the square wooden sand tower to the left.

The coaling facility shown in this photo of a Detroit, Toledo & Ironton 2-8-2 at Springfield, Ohio, in 1941, uses a bucket conveyor to deliver coal to the chute and apron, which can be swung out over the tender. A water column is nearby. This is about as simple as a permanent coaling installation can be.

(Paul Dunn photo, Jay Williams Collection)

When a permanent coaling station wasn't needed, the Fairfield Engineering Company of Marion, Ohio, sold a "Drag Conveyor" for use in transferring coal from hopper cars to locomotive tenders about anywhere the railroad wanted to do it. This photo shows such an operation at an unknown location on the Cloverleaf District of the Nickel Plate. The advertising sheet for this style of conveyor is shown on the next page (page 62).

(Jay Williams Collection)

THE FAIRFIELD MODEL A-201 DRAG CONVEYOR

(TROUGH 22" WIDE)

This Fairfield Conveyor can be used with or without a Fairfield Car Unloader or in a gravity feeding pit.

Built in lengths ranging from 25 to 35 feet; powered by electric motor or gasoline engine, designed for handling ALL sizes of bituminous and anthracite coal but can also be used for unloading coke and cinders.

Carefully proportioned construction provides rugged strength with no excess weight; skillful balance with exceptional boom overhang allows maximum clearance and storage.

Amply powered it is built to render maximum service at minimum cost. Guaranteed capacity 75 tons of coal per hour—actual capacity considerably in excess of this.

CONDENSED SPECIFICATIONS

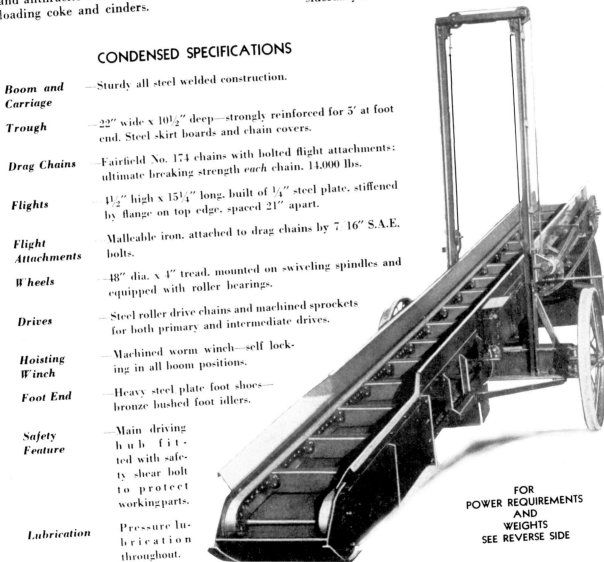

Boom and Carriage	—Sturdy all steel welded construction.
Trough	—22" wide x 10½" deep—strongly reinforced for 5' at foot end. Steel skirt boards and chain covers.
Drag Chains	—Fairfield No. 174 chains with bolted flight attachments; ultimate breaking strength *each* chain, 14,000 lbs.
Flights	—4½" high x 15¼" long, built of ¼" steel plate, stiffened by flange on top edge, spaced 21" apart.
Flight Attachments	—Malleable iron, attached to drag chains by 7/16" S.A.E. bolts.
Wheels	—48" dia. x 4" tread, mounted on swiveling spindles and equipped with roller bearings.
Drives	—Steel roller drive chains and machined sprockets for both primary and intermediate drives.
Hoisting Winch	—Machined worm winch—self locking in all boom positions.
Foot End	—Heavy steel plate foot shoes—bronze bushed foot idlers.
Safety Feature	—Main driving hub fitted with safety shear bolt to protect working parts.
Lubrication	—Pressure lubrication throughout.

FOR
POWER REQUIREMENTS
AND
WEIGHTS
SEE REVERSE SIDE

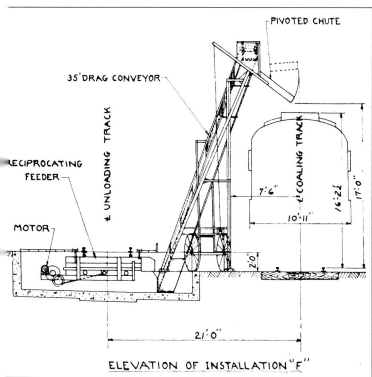

The Fairfield Engineering Company supplied its customers with a drawing that showed them how to place the conveyors. Three of those arrangements have been lifted from the drawing and reproduced here. In two of the drawings a reciprocating feeder is shown in a pit. One drawing shows the conveyor without any apparatus to feed it other than a slope, thus illustrating the versatility of the machinery. The drawing and catalog sheet are dated 1937.

(All drawings, C&O Historical Society Collection)

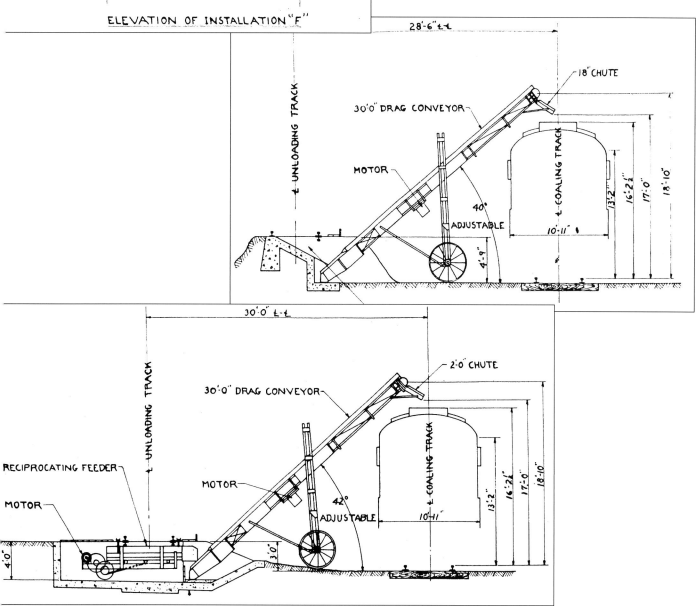

(*left*) This photo is lifted from an advertisement by the Ross & White Company of Chicago, in the 1929 edition of *Railway Engineering & Maintenance Cyclopedia* and shows that they were also offering "N&W Type" engine coalers. Again, those pictured were on the Virginian at Roanoke, Va.

(right) This Ross & White coaling station is actually an automatic coaler, not just a regular coaling station built in steel. Their definition was that if the coaler worked automatically to fuel locomotives it didn't matter if it dumped coal into a bin before it was discharged into a tender. The photo of the Grand Trunk coaling station near South Bend on page 52 of this book, is probably one of these.

(*above*) Ross & White also offered their "Red Devil" conveyor style engine coaler. The ad copy said "…the Red Devil Coaler shown saves its costs in labor alone every 90 days."

This Norfolk and Western coaling station at Vicker, Va. defies exact categorization, so it's placed in the automatic coaling section because the coal is delivered directly from hopper cars into locomotive tenders, through a trough slung under the bridge. This operation entailed shoving the loaded hoppers up a hill on a "balloon" track at left where they were spotted, they were then dropped down in pairs, using handbrakes as the coal was needed. After emptying the hoppers, they were again drifted, this time to the bottom of the "balloon" track at right and picked up by a local. Vicker is located about 35 miles west of Roanoke, near Walton. This unusual operation was replaced in 1952 by a concrete coaling tower which still stands as of this writing (2002).

(N&W Railway Phot

During the steam era not only did the railways have to contend with acquiring, moving, storing, and dispensing coal for their locomotives, but they had to collect and dispose of the cinder residue from the fireboxes, which were cleaned at the end of each run, usually at major terminals. Cinder pits were placed between the rails in the engine service area, and after they were dumped into these pits from the locomotive grates, they were moved by conveyor, clam shell, or bucket hoist systems into hopper cars to be carried away and disposed of as refuse or reused as ballast filler, or in some other manner. Cinder handling was automated at about the same time that mechanical coaling stations came into use. These much smaller machines were usually built by the same companies that built coaling stations. There is not a great variety in these plants beyond the three major types mentioned.

The cinder handling system at Hinton, W. Va., a major terminal on the C&O, consists of a skip-hoist bucket system with hoists leading from two locomotive servicing tracks and dumping to ash cars parked in the middle. Usually there is only one hoist, or two from the same side. The photo was taken in 1946.
(C&O railway Photo, C&O Historical Society collection)

This Wabash cinder conveyor is located in a very cramped engine servicing area in St. Louis. It uses the skip-hoist principal, as do almost all standard cinder plants.
(William Raia, Jay Williams Collection)

N & W TYPE
CINDER PLANT

Here you find the same strong, rigid construction, the same machinery and technical advantages, the same practical simplicity as in the Crane Type plant—with a different design for application wherever mainline overhead clearance for cinder car track is required.

Design demands a straight tower, with higher discharge, and a pivoted apron for lowering cinders.

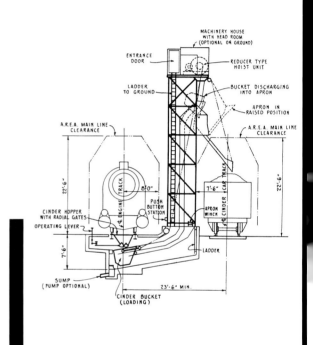

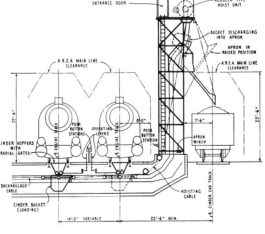

This Robertson & Schaefer catalog page illustrates with a photograph and drawings its N&W Type cinder conveyor. As explained in the ad copy this was intended for a higher discharge point, and had a straight tower.

CRANE TYPE CINDER PLANT

This simple, efficient, modern plant is a product of continuous study of practical railroad needs. A unit structure—assembled and welded in the shop, and machinery assembled in the shop—the plant arrives ready for erection, and can be easily erected by railroad workers.

Foundation—Shallow depth of pit with sufficient headroom for maintenance.

Track Centers—For plants with 50 cu. ft. bucket 23 ft.—for plants with 80 cu. ft. bucket 24 ft. (minimum dimension).

Tower—Rigid frame construction; main members, $\frac{5}{16}''$—bucket guides $\frac{3}{8}''$ minimum thickness. Bucket guides do not form part of the main structure—when worn, exchange guides only.

Machinery House—On top of tower; full protection of machinery and control switches at all times. No hinged-top lid covers. Optional: machinery house on ground.

Bucket—Skip hoist type—not rotary dump. Decreasing power demand when discharging. The load is discharged directly into the cinder car without baffle plate or apron. A special deflector plate in bucket prevents spilling when changing direction in guides. Scoop type shape—stronger than the conventional type, reinforced to distribute axle loads uniformly. Heavy square shafts with turned journals for wide thread, chilled rollers. Carrying and dump rollers in separate continuous guides—no switch-over to and from guides or dump cams.

Hopper—Cast iron heavy ribbed construction, non-warping; undercut radial gates easily opened and controlled. Positive gate stop prevents discharge without bucket underneath. Heavy duty type operating mechanism. Capacities up to 80 cubic feet.

Hoist Unit—Reducer with standard electric motor (no gear motor)—one set of spur gear and pinion for slow speed transmission to drum. Drum, machine scored, high test cast iron cable sheaves of large diameter. Extra flexible pre-formed hoisting cable.

Electric Control—Manual or Semi-automatic.

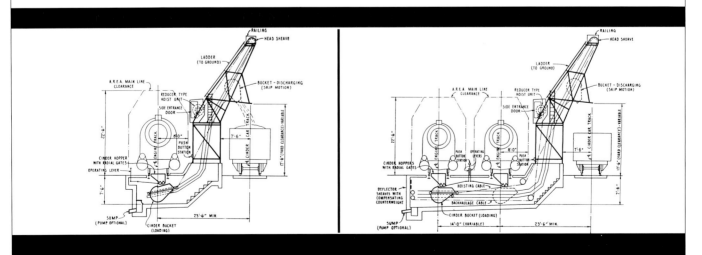

Another Robertson & Schaefer catalog page shows the company's Crane type cinder plant with a gantry arm that reached out over the cinder car track to dump its skip-hoist car. The drawings show the actual function.

A crane type cinder plant makes up an important part of the engine terminal facility on the C&O at Columbus, Ohio in this July 1948 view. A cinder carrying hopper car is spotted under the crane, ready to receive another load from the skip-hoist bucket. Since the bucket isn't visible, it is in the tunnel under the pits to receive a load of cinders. The cinders were knocked out of the locomotive ash pan into the pit which had a hopper bottom. This hopper then dumped into the buckets which traveled out a tunnel, up the crane and were tipped into the waiting cinder car. Some railroads had dedicated cinder cars (usually old hopper cars which had outlived their revenue-producing lives, while others used ordinary cars out of revenue service, as needed.

(C&O Ry Photo, C&O Historical Society Collection).

(below) This tiny photograph, lifted from *Railway Engineering & Maintenance Cyclopedia* for 1929, shows a concrete cinder plant built by Ogle. It served two tracks, whose discharge pits are to its immediate left. The plant sent its cinders through a chute and apron arrangement to the waiting cars at right.

Another crane type cinder hoist is seen in this overhead view of the C&O engine terminal on its Big Sandy coal fields line at Shelby, Kentucky in 1950. The bucket is a very thin curved vehicle, quite unlike most cinder-carrying buckets, and is in the full discharge position, a stack of cinders starting to fill the first of four hoppers in line. The end markings on the nearest car identify it as C261, indicating it's a car in dedicated cinder service.

(C&O Ry Photo, C&O Historical Society Collection)

This Fairbanks, Morse "Universal" cinder conveyor was designed for serving multiple tracks. The buckets were available in 40, 60, and 80 cubic foot sizes. This design had a self-contained motor-driven hoist mounted in the small machinery house on the tower. Push-button stations were mounted conveniently on the side of the tower. When the operator pressed the "start" button the hoist drew the bucket to the "dump" position, discharging the cinders. It stayed in this position until the "start" button was pressed, and the cycle was repeated.

(From Fairbanks, Morse 1939 catalog).

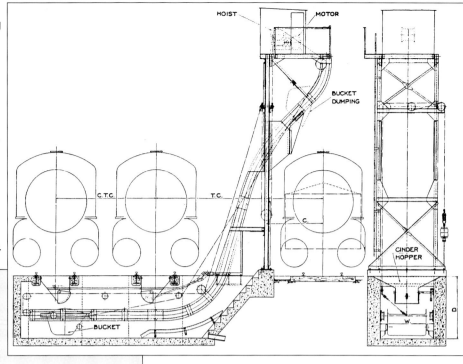

(above) This FM Universal cinder plant is seen in a 1953 photo on the C&O at Martin, Kentucky. It served a single track with two pits, which are visible near the concrete slabs and hand rails. A line of the C&O's dedicated cinder cars waits to be filled. Note the electrical lines coming into the hoist-house at the top of the tower, and the several lights to ensure proper illumination at night.

(right) A view of the same facility with the pit tracks showing.

(both, C&O Ry, C&O Historical Society Collection)

(above) William Robertson & Company of Chicago was also a large supplier of cinder conveyors. The photo at left is taken from one of their catalog sheets from the late 1920s, showing an arrangement for two buckets. Unlike other systems, the buckets didn't tip up to dump, but had drop bottoms. This made the hoisting tower very simple in layout.

The Robertson catalog sheet also carried this illustration of four conveyors installed on tracks leading to a large roundhouse. They didn't identify the railroad or location.

This drawing is also lifted from the catalog sheet and shows the specifications and dimensions of the facility in elevation.

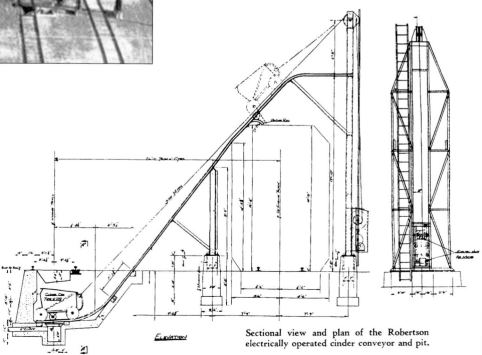

Sectional view and plan of the Robertson electrically operated cinder conveyor and pit.

The illustrations at left are taken from the *RE&M Cyclopedia* 1929 again and show the standard ash handling equipment approved by the American Railway Engineering Association. The mechanical types have been covered in the previous pages. The pit with track iron columns, where ashes are simply shoveled out by hand, is the simplest type. The depressed ash car track, another style, allows the ashes to fall into the car directly. The large drawing showing the Water Pit style was recommended for terminals with turn-around of 50-160 engines per day.

The small photo at bottom is the best illustration (again from the 1929 *RE&M Cyclopedia*) we could locate showing the large terminal Water Pit style. Troughs of water were located next to where the locomotive fires were cleaned. The cinders dropped into the water and were quenched. They were then removed periodically by the moving overhead clamshell crane. In other instances they could be removed by a locomotive crane traveling on one of the adjacent tracks, as shown by the illustration at right.

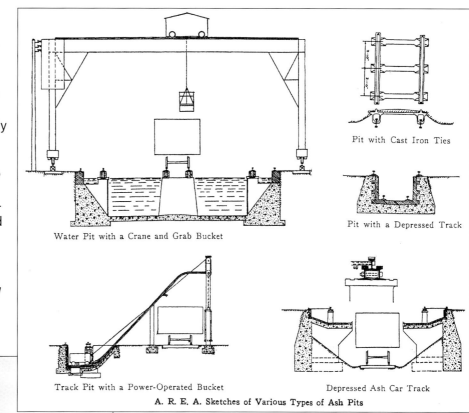

Water Pit with a Crane and Grab Bucket

Pit with Cast Iron Ties

Pit with a Depressed Track

Track Pit with a Power-Operated Bucket

Depressed Ash Car Track

A. R. E. A. Sketches of Various Types of Ash Pits

(right) C&NW's Galena roundhouse in Chicago uses an overhead crane to lift cinders from shallow between-rails pits and place them in cars located on center tracks. This system was much less used than the mechanical plants.

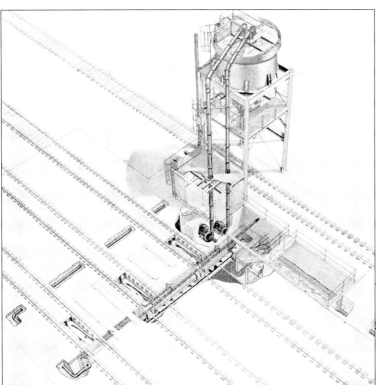

Very late in the steam era the United Conveyor Corporation, which had been supplying cinder disposal systems for industrial power plants, decided to make available an ultra-modern disposal system for railroads. By the time this appeared, railroads are frantically dieselizing, and as far as this author can determine this system was installed only on the Norfolk and Western at Williamson, W. Va., and Portsmouth, Ohio.

In the United system the ashes were dropped into an underground trench where they are washed into a sluice trough by high-pressure water jets. Gravity carried the ash-laden water to a sump and pumped it to an overhead drying bin. The water was then re-used and the dried ashes dumped vertically into waiting cars.

The illustration on the right shows the action inside the United locomotive ash pit, with its jets of high-pressure water washing dumped ashes into the sluiceway.

(both illustrations from 1948 RE&M Cyclopedia)

This 1946 overhead view of the ash-handling area of N&W's Williamson, W. Va. terminal shows the United system's above ground components including the elevated pipes, ash drying ("de-watering" according to United ads) bin, and the concrete pads under which the pits and sluices ran.

(N&W, Kenneth L. Miller Collection)

Early Diesel Locomotive Fueling Facilities

I have allowed less than 10 per cent of this book for discussion and illustration of diesel locomotive fueling stations because they deserve their own more extensive treatment. This will be a very brief overview of their development and illustration of a couple of case-specific examples. Since the introduction of diesels on American railroads was, for the most part, incremental, most roads were faced with having to serve two types of motive power for a period of years. For some of the earlier diesel users this was as much as 20 years, for others it was usually within 10 years. Because of this incremental change many railroads simply adapted steam facilities by adding hoses, pipes, and tanks in existing operations. Other lines took the philosophy that entirely new diesel fueling stations should be built.

In the early decades of dieselization the railroads that adapted rather than building new dedicated facilities dominated, and thus the variety of fueling facilities was great. The fuel oil itself was delivered in tank cars, and these were often used as the storage vehicle from which the fuel was dispensed as well as for transportation, and many railroads had fleets of tank cars dedicated to company diesel fuel use. In other instances storage tanks of medium or large capacity were built and the fuel pumped from the cars into them and then used in locomotive fueling as needed. These two approaches mirror, in many ways, the difference between the steam locomotive elevated mechanical coaling station with large storage bin and the automatic coalers.

Illustrated on the next few pages are some general examples and two locations on the C&O that can serve as archetypes to many elsewhere with only slight difference.

This Southern Railway multiple-track servicing station is a good example of the newly built dedicated installation specifically designed for diesel fueling. Like all fueling stations, it has a profusion of stanchions for holding pipes and hoses, elevated gangways for employees to walk while connecting hoses and nozzles, all set on

concrete slabs. The length of the station and number of fueling positions was dictated by the number of coupled units that could be expected to arrive for service. Unlike steam locomotives, which operated as independent units, diesels were strung together, and it would have been inefficient to have to fuel each unit separately (from 1955 edition of *Railway Track & Structures Cyclopedia* (RT&SC).

This new but fairly simple facility employs a series of stand-pipes with dispensing arms and nozzles for both fuel and water on the Santa Fe. This photo from the 1955 edition of RT&SC.

(above) This New York Central facility was illustrated at night to show the importance of good lighting for fueling stations to avoid waste and promote safety. The lights were of the explosion proof type. Each counter-weighted fueling mast extends from its own pump housing. (both from 1955 RT&SC)

(left) Another Santa Fe facility uses pipes attached to tall masts. The counterweight on the mast causes the hose to retract when not in use.

(*left*) Self-contained, semi-portable fueling pumps were offered by the Bowser Company. These pumping stations had the pump, meter, fuel filter & hose all encased in a steel cabinet, and could be moved to different locations and used seasonally, intermittently, etc. Of course, they would still have to have a source of fuel from a tank car or highway truck.
(*1955 RT&SC*)

(*right*) The 1955 RT&SC illustrated these switch engines being fueled by a highway tanker truck to show how efficiency could be gained by delivering fuel to such locomotives at their work area on the yard rather than having them come to the main terminal to be fueled.

This fueling station was built by Bowser, Inc., for the Erie Railroad at Marion, Ohio. It consisted of four 25,000 gallon fuel oil tanks, two 300 gallon-per-minute oil pumps, four locomotive fueling locations. The piping was arranged so that the pumps could deliver fuel from tank cars to storage or from storage to locomotives. The facility also had four 6,000 gallon tanks for lubricating oils.
(*Jay Williams Collection*)

The two photos and drawing illustrate the fueling masts at Rainelle, W. Va. designed and installed by the C&O's engineering department in 1955. This style of fueling arm used a short, short counterbalanced arm holding a short hose, attached to a short mast. It was set on a concrete base. This is a good example of a simple diesel fueling station for a small terminal. The fuel was initially drawn from tank cars directly, but then a tank was installed (see next page)

(all C&O Photos)

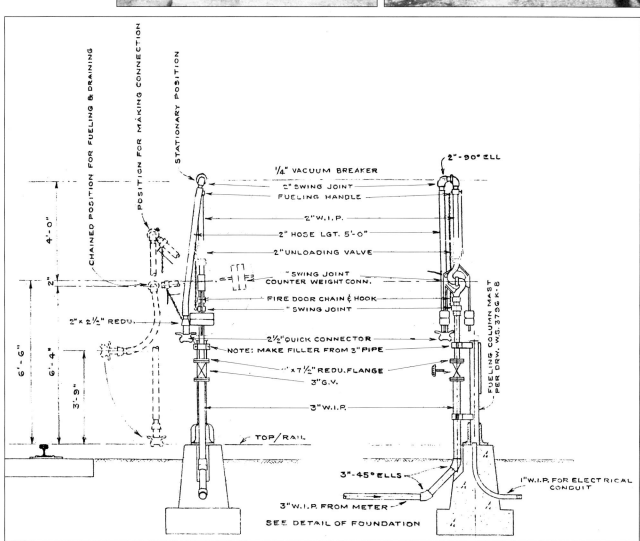

CHAINED POSITION FOR FUELING & DRAINING

POSITION FOR MAKING CONNECTION

STATIONARY POSITION

4'-0"

2"

6'-6"

6'-4"

3'-9"

2"x 2½" REDU.

1/4" VACUUM BREAKER

2"-90° ELL

2" SWING JOINT

FUELING HANDLE

2" W.I.P.

2" HOSE LGT. 5'-0"

2" UNLOADING VALVE

" SWING JOINT
COUNTER WEIGHT CONN.

FIRE DOOR CHAIN & HOOK

" SWING JOINT

2½" QUICK CONNECTOR

NOTE: MAKE FILLER FROM 3" PIPE

" x 7½" REDU. FLANGE

3" G.V.

3" W.I.P.

FUELING COLUMN MAST
PER DRW. W.S. 379 G K-8

TOP/RAIL

3"-45° ELLS

I" W.I.P. FOR ELECTRICAL
CONDUIT

3" W.I.P. FROM METER

SEE DETAIL OF FOUNDATION

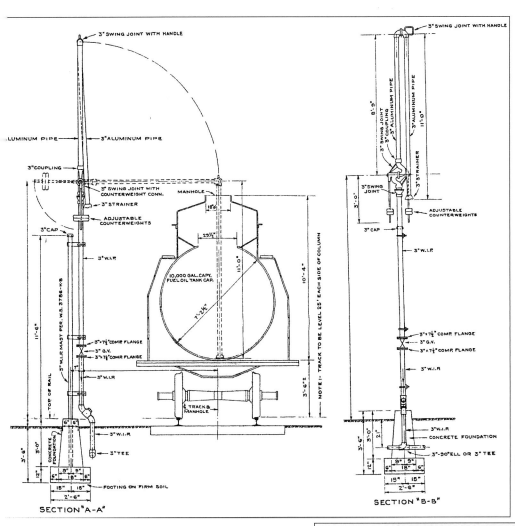

The drawing on the left shows the C&O's standard 3-inch unloading column for diesel fuel tank cars. These arms were used in pumping the fuel from the arriving tank cars directly to locomotives or into holding tanks.

(C&O Historical Society Collection)

(*below*) Tank cars being unloaded at Rainelle, W. Va., 1955

(C&O Railway Photo)

(*below*) String of tank cars being unloaded at Clifton Forge, Va. 1955.

(C&O Ry Photo, C&O Historical Society Collection)

The photo and drawings on this page depict the 30,492 gallon (!) diesel fuel storage tank and Rainelle, W. Va. The tank was placed in a clay dike or revetment to prevent spillage in case of rupture, and had a steel frame pump house positioned next to it.

(Photo and drawings by C&O Railway, 1955)

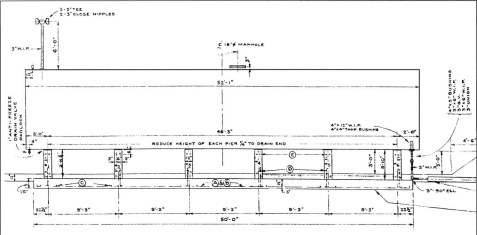

Drawing shows the tank's side and end views are shown above and right. Below is the steel pump house and the walkway over the dike at right.

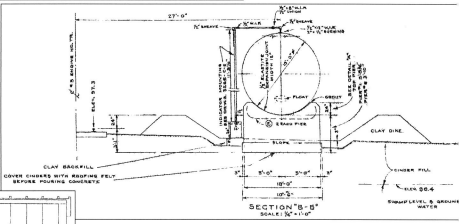

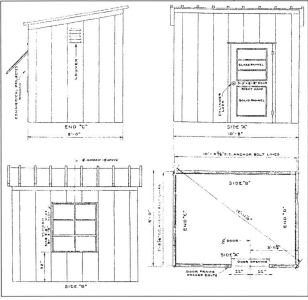

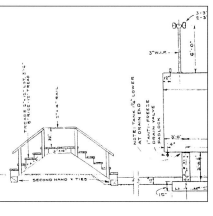

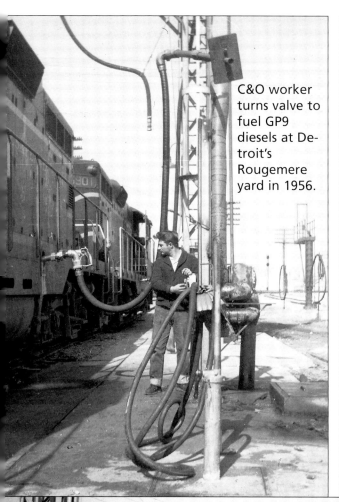

C&O worker turns valve to fuel GP9 diesels at Detroit's Rougemere yard in 1956.

Fueling mast (nearest) and unloading column (behind) allow C&O terminal workers at Newport News, Va. to unload fuel or to fuel locomotives on adjacent tracks.

(left) Tank car unloading area and diesel fueling station at Rougemere yard in Detroit. Very heavy columns hold cantilevered catwalks and unloading hoses. In front of them are the fueling masts for pumping the diesel oil into locomotives. There is a wonderful profusion of spare hoses hanging on various poles.

right) This interesting view shows the fuel unloading track at Newport News, Va. with six of the standard C&O 3-inch unloading columns with no tank cars present. The large tank to the right, just visible in the photo, is for storing the unloaded oil.

(all C&O Railway)

BOWSER, INC.

1369 Creighton Avenue, Fort Wayne 2, Indiana
Products and Sales Offices are listed in the Classified Indexes

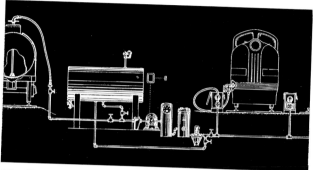

The illustration above shows a typical combination installation for locomotive fueling and tank car unloading. Both jobs are handled by the same meter and power pump. Many other variations are possible.

THE PIONEER MAKER OF EQUIPMENT FOR RAILROAD LIQUIDS

Fueling Systems for Diesels

Bowser fueling systems are available in a variety of types and capacities for any railroad fueling requirement. High capacity systems for terminal multi-fueling, smaller ones for a single locomotive, a switcher, section work cars or scooters . . . are all in service every day on most railroads.

Meters of large or small capacity, with verified and printed tickets when desired, show the exact quantity measured.

One-Package Fueling Unit

Bowser Serv-A-Trains are self-contained units in attractive, sturdy cabinets for accurately dispensing either fuel or lubricating oils. They are quickly and easily installed, easily moved to other locations, because there are only two connections—the suction and the electric power.

Available in capacities of 50 or 100 g.p.m. for diesel fuel and 12 g.p.m. for lubricating oil. Fifty feet of hose with power-driven hose reel—easy-to-read dial—ticket printer available at extra cost.

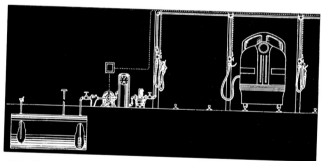

This illustration shows a system for dispensing lubricating oil to the supply tank on a diesel engine. Hose reels may be substituted for the wall hose hangers. A number of other methods are available, depending on the requirement.

Lubricating Oil Systems

Complete metering systems are provided to accurately deliver lubricating oil direct to diesel engine crankcases. They are complete with hose reel for double-quick service and can be equipped with ticket printers to record each delivery.

Other Bowser systems unload and measure lube oil from incoming tank cars or drums. Complete Bowser installations for handling used oil drained from diesel crankcases are also used by many railroads.

COMPLETE ENGINEERING SERVICE

As the pioneer maker of equipment for handling railroad liquids of all types, Bowser is prepared to furnish capable and dependable engineering service. By supplying all the equipment necessary for proper installation, you are assured of complete satisfaction because Bowser assumes the entire responsibility.

By 1952 when the *Railway Supply Industry Yearbook* was issued, no one was offering anything to support steam locomotives. Bowser, Inc. was, however, advertising its services and products for servicing diesels.